Adversity Is Your Greatest Ally

How to Use Life's Challenges as Stepping Stones to Live the Life of Your Dreams

By
Coach Michael Taylor

Published by Creation Publishing Group LLC

www.creationpublishing.com

© 2015 Michael Taylor

ISBN # 978-0-9641894-6-1

Library of Congress Number # 2015907513

All rights reserved. No part of this book may be used or reproduced, stored in, or introduced into, a retrieval system, or transmitted in any form or by any means without the express written consent of the publisher.

Published and printed in the United States of America.

Table of contents

Acknowledgements
Introduction
Chapter 1: Adversity
Chapter 2: Who Are You?
Chapter 3: Make Peace with Your Past
Chapter 4: Intuition/Synchronicity
Chapter 5: Cultural Conditioning/Programming
Chapter 6: The Hero's Journey
Chapter 7: The Breakdown Breakthrough Principle
Chapter 8: The Power of Purpose
Chapter 9: Your Heart's Desire
Chapter 10: Living With Joy
Resources
About the Author

Acknowledgements

First, foremost and always, I must acknowledge the energy and intelligence that created and is still creating this amazing Universe. This energy and intelligence is the Source of my wisdom, my passion, my creativity, and my drive to do my part in making the world a better place. To my Source I simply say thank you. Thank you for this amazing gift called life, and thank you for all the experiences that have brought me to this point in my life where I feel happy, whole, and joyful. In addition, I feel powerful, confident, and secure that I am fulfilling my divine purpose, and I'm now ready to be on an international stage sharing my truth and changing the world.

As I reflect back over all the adversities I had to overcome, I recognize that I was never alone, and I am aware that it was that still small voice within me that supported and guided me in turning my adversities into allies. I am eternally grateful for the trust and understanding I've developed with my Source, and it provides me with unwavering faith and a deep sense of gratitude that I am connected to a power greater than myself that is always just a thought and a feeling away.

So I simply say, thank you Source, for your unconditional love and support, and for providing me with everything I need to live an extraordinary life.

I will always remember this quote; "Who I am is God's gift to me. What I make of myself is my gift to God."

I know you are going to love my gifts back to you!

To: Dr. Wayne Dyer

Although you are no longer with us, I wanted to thank you for teaching me how to think and for helping me to understand that as a human being I have the capacity to accomplish anything any other human being has ever accomplished. It is this simple yet powerful concept that has allowed me to trust my inner wisdom and create the life of my dreams. Your wisdom will live on and continue to have a deep influence on my life, and I am grateful to have had the opportunity to meet you and embrace you. Your teachings have been instrumental in my spiritual growth and I am forever indebted to you for your wisdom. Rest in peace and continue shining your light, wherever you are.

To: Neale Donald Walsch

Thank you for being the spiritual conduit that confirmed what I had always believed about God. God is love and I am an expression of that love. Your *Conversations With God* books were instrumental in helping me overcome a lot of adversities in my life. I accepted your challenge of becoming the grandest version of the greatest vision I held for myself as a human being, and I am committed to walking hand-in-hand with you to help heal humanity.

To: Mike Dooley

Thank you for *The Notes From The Universe*. I read them every single day and their messages always fill me with insight and inspiration. Many times your Notes were the perfect nudge I needed to push me through adversity in my life, and I recognize that The Notes that you write come from the same source that inspired this book.

You rock sir!

To: Marianne Williamson

Thank you for putting me on a path to *A Return To Love*. Your wisdom and compassion inspires me. Your lessons from *A Course In Miracles* were instrumental in my transformation and growth. Thank you for challenging me to look at my greatest fear and for helping me understand that I actually had nothing to be afraid of.

To: Les Brown

Thank you for modeling what a motivational speaker should be like. You are one of the reasons I stepped into this field of infinite possibilities. I will never forget you taking the time to speak with me on the phone and encouraging me to live my dreams. I'm following in your footsteps, sir, and at the same time I am blazing my own trail.

To: Deepak Chopra

Thank you for your ancient wisdom and your ability to challenge my intellect to look deeper into the nature of reality. Your books and programs were instrumental in shaping my spiritual beliefs about the Universe and they have guided me to always look deeper and trust the Divine Intelligence that orchestrates the Cosmos.

To: Mrs. B.

I am so glad I found you and chose you to be my life partner. You exude unconditional love and your belief in me has definitely made this journey a lot easier. I absolutely love being married to you and I am so excited about our future. Thank you for loving me for the man that I am, and for simply being the amazing woman that you are. You are absolutely perfect for me! I Love You!

Introduction

In case you haven't noticed, life is filled with adversities. We are constantly faced with challenges that are usually unplanned, and more often than not, they can throw our lives into a tailspin that can be extremely difficult to get out of.

After facing and overcoming a multiplicity of adversities in my own life, I have now come to the conclusion that life isn't supposed to be so difficult. As a matter of fact, I now fervently believe that life is supposed to be a joyful, rewarding, and fulfilling experience filled with great relationships, dynamic health, financial abundance, and a deep feeling of inner peace and serenity.

Unfortunately, most people seldom experience life in this way. Too many people experience painful relationships and a lack of financial resources, and they are so overwhelmed with stress that they have to rely on drugs and alcohol just to try to cope.

So what about you? Are you experiencing your life as joyful and rewarding? Or are you experiencing life as a stressful event, filled with scarcity and lack?

No matter where you are in life right now, rest assured that it is possible for you to create a life that is filled with everything you can imagine. In order to do this, you must recognize that there will always be mountains in your way, but if you have the proper tools it can make climbing those mountains a heck of a lot easier.

You see, mountains are great metaphors for adversity. We will always have mountains to climb, but if we prepare ourselves and even look forward to climbing those mountains, there isn't an obstacle that we can't overcome. The key is preparation.

This book is written to prepare you to face all of the mountains in your life. If I can overcome being a high school dropout, divorce, bankruptcy, foreclosure, and depression, and become a successful entrepreneur, author, motivational speaker, and radio show host, then I know with absolute certainty that you can overcome any adversity you may be dealing with.

So rest assured that you already have everything you need to climb the mountains in your life. When you combine your commitment, patience, perseverance, and persistence with the wisdom contained in this book, you will have everything you need to use your life challenges as stepping-stones to live the life of your dreams.

Let's go climb some mountains!

Coach Michael Taylor

"All the adversity I've had in my life, all my troubles and obstacles, have strengthened me...You may not realize it when it happens, but a kick in the teeth may be the best thing in the world for you."

Walt Disney

Chapter 1
Adversity

If you're reading this book, chances are you've experienced some difficulties and challenges in your own life and you're possibly looking for ways to deal with those challenges. Rest assured that no matter what you may be going through (or have already gone through) there is definitely light at the end of the tunnel. As a matter of fact, if you accept the fact that you are "the light" already, then you're already half way home.

This isn't just some new age *airy-fairy* expression. It is a scientifically proven fact. Whether you are aware of it or not, you are the light! Or, if that is too difficult to grasp, simply accept that the light is in you. If you really want to overcome the adversities in your life, the best place to start is to recognize that there is something inside of you that can support you in overcoming any obstacle that shows up. You can call it "the light", divine energy, reason and intellect, God, or whatever you choose to call it. The key is for you to acknowledge it and accept that it is available to you. Once you access it and learn to trust it, you will have everything you need to deal with any adversity you have to face.

In our current culture we have been taught to believe that adversity is a "bad" thing, and we therefore try to avoid it at all costs. But what if adversity was good? What if it is simply preparation for something remarkable that is about to occur?

Shakespeare said it best when he stated "Nothing is either good or bad until you think it so."

I'd like for you to think of adversity as simply stepping-stones to live the life of your dreams. They are neither good nor bad, until you choose to label them as such. My hope is that the content in this book will help you face and deal with the adversity in your life, and you will hopefully learn how to turn those adversities into allies which will support you in living the life you know you are capable of living.

The information that I will be sharing in this book isn't based on some academic theory. It is based on my own life experiences of overcoming being born in the inner city projects of Corpus Christi Texas to a single mother with six kids who were the poster children for poverty back in the sixties. It is based on my ability to overcome being a high school dropout who refused to succumb to a life of mediocrity, was able to climb the corporate ladder, and become a mid-level manager for a multi-million dollar company at the tender age of 22. It is also based on my ability to overcome divorce, bankruptcy, foreclosure, and a deep state of depression in which I even contemplated taking my own life.

So when it comes to adversity, I know a thing or two about overcoming them, and I would like to share some lessons I've learned that I know can help you overcome the adversities in your own life.

So are you ready? Are you ready to turn your adversities into allies so that you can live the life of your dreams? If you are, then I must begin with some good news and some bad news.

The bad news is, life happens and challenges *definitely* happen. There is no getting around the fact that you will eventually have to deal with some adversity in your life. The good news is, you have everything you need right now to overcome any challenge or obstacle that's put in front of you. And so my job is to share some information, wisdom, and insights that can hopefully support you in moving past those challenges and living the life I know you're capable of living.

So if you're ready, I'd like to begin by sharing *The 5 Keys to Turn Adversities Into Allies*.

The first thing we want to do is define adversity. What exactly is it? *Webster's Dictionary* says that adversity is "a state or instance of serious or continued difficulty or misfortune."

Do you relate to this statement? Have you ever experienced a state or instance of serious or continued difficulty or misfortune? I know I have, and I'm pretty sure that I will experience more in the future. But what I know with absolute certainty is, no matter what adversity I'll have to deal with in the future, I am confident that I will be able to handle them and move past them.

Life is full of adversities, but it's been said that it's not what happens to you, it's what you *do* with what happens to you that really matters. And so that is the attitude I want you to take as you're reading this book, because stuff happens, but it's how you react to that stuff which determines whether or not you become a victor or a victim; and I want you to be a victor.

So let's take a look at some people who have overcome adversities in their own lives, and look at the end result.

For example, Bill Gates, who happens to be the richest man on the planet; did you know that when he started his first business it failed? Did you also know that he is a college dropout? So he's obviously experienced adversity in his life - but look at where he ended up.

Or how about Albert Einstein, who in my mind is one of the most brilliant scientists who's ever lived. Did you know he didn't speak until he was four years old, and his parents were concerned that there was something wrong with him? They didn't think he was really that smart. But we all know the story - he was definitely a brilliant, brilliant man who overcame several adversities in his own life and left a powerful legacy with his brilliance.

And then there is Jim Carrey, who is one, if not the highest paid comedian, on the planet who has received $20-25 million to be featured in a movie. There was a time in his life when his family had to live in a trailer and he actually became homeless for a while.

Did you know that Benjamin Franklin dropped out of school at the age of ten? A brilliant man who literally changed the world with his wisdom, although he dropped out of school at such an early age.

And then there's Stephen King, who is the famous horror writer whose first novel was rejected more than thirty times, and now he's one of the most premier writers of horror ever.

And then there's Oprah Winfrey, who runs a billion-dollar, multi-media empire. What you may not know is that she was raped and molested as a child; and at just fourteen, she gave birth to a child who eventually died.

She's overcome some really amazing adversities in her life, and look where she ended up.

And then there's Steven Spielberg, who is one of my favorite directors, and creator of several of my favorite movies. Did you know that he was actually rejected from film school at USC because they didn't think he had the talent to be a good filmmaker? Look how he turned out!

Or what about Jay Z, the famous rapper who's now worth something in the region of $500 million dollars and is a partner with, and married to, Beyoncé, one of the most beautiful and talented entertainers in the world. Jay Z attempted to get a contract signed for rapping and he was rejected several times; nobody wanted him, so he started his own label. Now he's one of the most successful rappers, producers, media moguls, and businessmen in the world.

Have you noticed the pattern? Each of these people went through different levels of adversity, and they were still able to overcome them and eventually become successful.

You might be saying to yourself, "but these people are famous." Well guess what? They didn't start out that way. They started out with lots of adversity in their lives, but they refused to let it keep them from creating the life of their dreams.

The only difference between you and these "famous" people is that they had a vision for their lives, and they made a commitment to fulfilling that vision - and they didn't allow adversity to keep them from doing what they knew they were capable of accomplishing.

Rest assured that you too have everything you need right now to overcome any adversity placed in front of you. The two questions you must now ask yourself are, *what do I want?* And *what am I willing to do to get it?* When you can sufficiently answer these two questions you are ready to begin moving towards your destiny. The problem is, very few people can answer these two simple questions. Can you? Do you know exactly what you want? Do you have a vision of how you want your life to turn out? It all begins with making a decision and becoming clear on exactly what you want and then being willing to do whatever it takes to get what you want.

I'll talk more about this in the upcoming chapter on Dreams, but for now I want to focus on the *5 Keys To Turning Adversities Into Allies* because it is going to lay the foundation for everything else in this book. Once you fully understand these five keys, you will have some tools that will support you in dealing with adversity and they should help you overcome all the challenges in your life.

Key 1: You must be willing to take 100 percent responsibility for your life.

That's it! If you are unwilling to do this you might as well stop reading this book right now. Your success relies on your willingness to take 100 percent responsibility for your life and everything that happens to you. You can't blame your parents, where you were born, or the color of your skin. You can't blame your lack of education, your ex-spouse, or your age. **You** must decide that you're going to take 100 percent responsibility for your life, and then make it happen.

Are you willing to do this?

Of course, this does not mean that there won't be people who may hurt you, lie to you, or betray you. It does not mean that there won't be times when you are tired, frustrated, angry, confused, and simply want to give up. It also doesn't mean that there won't be times where you might try to place blame on the government, society, religion, or the particular culture you were brought up in for being the cause of your failure.

It means you are making a conscious decision, right now, that you are willing to do whatever it takes, and you recognize that if you do not assume 100 percent responsibility for your life, you literally give up your power.

A good way to do this is to remember the Three C's. Choice, Chance, and Change. It all begins with you first and foremost making the choice that you will take 100 percent responsibility for your life to turn out the way you want it to. And then you must make the *choice* to take the *chance* that you can then *change* your life.

Of course, this takes some risk, but with huge risk comes huge reward, and you must take a chance if you want anything in your life to change.

Make the choice to take a chance if you want your life to change. **Choose right now!**

So, that's the first key to turn adversities into allies: **Take 100 percent responsibility for your life.**

Key 2: **You must be willing to get out of your comfort zone.**

Another way to look at getting out of your comfort zone is simply being willing to face your fears. It's been said that fear is the destroyer of dreams, and if you aren't willing to address your fears, you will never be able to accomplish anything of significance.

There is a wonderful quote that states: "You must realize, that fear is not real. It is a product of thoughts you create. Do not misunderstand me, danger is very real, but fear is a choice."

Fear is a choice. You can choose to let it keep you from accomplishing your goals, or you can feel the fear and do it any way. A powerful acronym for fear is *False Experiences Appearing Real*, which means they are simply thoughts in your mind that appear to be real, yet, they are simply figments of your imagination. They only exist within the framework of your own mind. Getting out of your comfort zone means you learn to recognize your fears, and don't let them stop you from accomplishing your goals.

Getting out of your comfort zone means being willing to be uncomfortable. As a matter of fact, you must learn to become comfortable with being uncomfortable, if you truly want to accomplish extraordinary things in your life.

Key 3: **You must commit to your own growth.**

As a human being you have an infinite capacity for learning, and if you're not willing to learn, no one can help you; but if you are determined to learn, no one can stop you either. It is absolutely imperative that you make a commitment to growth. There's a wonderful saying that goes, "If you aren't growing, you're dying." So make a commitment to constant and never-ending improvement, and I can assure you, you'll be able to turn your adversities into allies.

Another way to look at growth is using the computer as a metaphor for your brain. A computer is an amazing technological machine that can be used to do remarkable things. To improve the performance of a computer you must constantly upgrade software and replace hardware to keep it running at its maximum potential. Your brain is more powerful than any computer, and you must be willing to constantly upgrade your internal software and take care of your hardware to keep it, too, running at its maximum potential.

Upgrading your inner software means that you are willing to look at the subconscious beliefs that may be limiting your potential. It also means that you are willing to add new programs (beliefs) that can support you in your growth. You can accomplish this by reading books and participating in classes that provide you with the knowledge to accomplish your goals and support you in feeling better about yourself as a human being.

The key is to commit to constant and never-ending improvement in all areas of your life.

Key 4: **You must develop a positive attitude.**

So what exactly is attitude? My definition of attitude is, "The compilation and expression of your beliefs, thoughts, and feelings."

If you have negative beliefs, thoughts, and feelings, you're going to have a negative attitude. If you have positive beliefs, thoughts, and feelings, you're going to have a positive attitude. So if you're truly committed to turning your adversities into allies, one of the things you have to do is to develop a positive attitude; because whenever life throws challenges at you, if you have a negative attitude, guess what happens? It's going to make things more difficult for you to deal with. But, if you maintain a positive attitude, and if you maintain the idea that it is absolutely possible for you to overcome challenges in your life, then it's going to be much easier for you to turn your adversities into allies. Developing a positive mental attitude is paramount to your success.

Key 5: **You must discover your unique gifts and talents.**

Whether you believe this or not, you have very special unique gifts and talents. Chances are, you have forgotten what they are, and more than likely you've given up on sharing them with the world - but rest assured they are within you. Your goal is to discover these gifts and talents, and reignite the inner flame of passion that will allow you to express them. Your gifts are not necessarily something you do - they are primarily about *who you are*. For example, being loving and caring is a gift. Being intelligent and analytical is also a gift. Being ambitious, driven, creative and extraverted, or being introverted and compassionate is a gift.

When you discover your gifts and apply them to your talents, then you will find your true purpose in life. If your gifts are being loving and caring, then your talent could lead you to be a healer or a member of the clergy. If your gifts include being intelligent and analytical, then your talent could lead you to become a doctor or a lawyer. If your gifts include being ambitious and driven, then you may become an entrepreneur or a manager. If you are creative and extraverted, chances are you will become some type of entertainer, and if you are introverted and compassionate, then you may choose to become a therapist or counselor.

Get the picture?

Your gifts are lying dormant within you. It is your responsibility to wake them up. No one can discover or express them for you, you must commit to discovering them for yourself. When you do, I can assure you that you will not only be able to fully express yourself authentically, but you will also be able to find joy and passion in everything you do.

Find your gifts and express your talents and you can live a rewarding and fulfilling life.

So to recap, the 5 Keys To Turn Adversities Into Allies are:

1: Take 100 percent responsibility for your life.
2: Get out of your comfort zone.
3: You must commit to your own growth.
4: You must develop a positive attitude.
5: You must discover your unique gifts and talents.

The final part of dealing with adversity is to develop an *attitude of gratitude*. Which means that you count your blessings for what you have, and not focus your attention on what you don't have. No matter how difficult your life might be right now, or how many challenges you may be faced with, rest assured that there is always, *always* something to be thankful for.

If you want to turn your adversities into allies, you must make a commitment to developing an *attitude of gratitude*. A simple way to do this is by simply writing down five things that you're grateful for every single day. That's it. Just start a journal, and each day take a few minutes to make a list of five things you're grateful for. Don't overthink it, just make a list. For example, your list might look like this:

I'm grateful that:
1. I woke up this morning.
2. I have a nice bed to sleep in.
3. My wife loves me.
4. I have a job.
5. I have food in my refrigerator.

You get to choose what you're grateful for, and it's up to you to think about it and write them down, but be sure to choose five different things you're grateful for each day. It's also a good idea to write your list right before you go to bed, or first thing in the morning. It will relax you and actually help you sleep better at night if you choose to do it before bed.

If you commit to doing this for 21 days straight, I can promise you that your attitude will shift for the better and you will find more things that you are grateful for. It takes around 21 days to form a new habit, but once you do, it becomes second nature. It may be a little difficult to begin with, but it gets easier with time, and eventually you will learn to love doing it.

Adversity

One of the reasons so many people experience adversity in their lives is because it's what they focus on all the time. If you focus all your attention on what's wrong with your life, more things that are wrong will show up. But, if you begin shifting your attitude to one of gratitude, you will begin to experience more things you're grateful for.

And so I would like to close this chapter by sharing something that I wrote as a result of my own 20-year journey of overcoming some seemingly insurmountable obstacles and adversities in my own life.

It's aptly titled, **Gratitude.**

> *"After more than 20 years of overcoming failure, heartbreak, betrayal, disappointment, and a long list of other adversities, I realize that right now in this very moment, I am happier now than I've ever been in my life. I am grateful for every adversity that I've ever faced, because I realize that they have shaped and molded me into the man I am today. If I had to do it all over again, I wouldn't change a thing because I turned my adversities into allies, and each one of them brought me a gift that blessed me in some way, even when I didn't understand it at that time.*
>
> *So I sit here in deep humility and gratitude for this amazing gift called life, and my hope is that my work and my message inspires you to have a similar experience that allows you to feel the connection, awe, and gratitude of this divine and sacred gift called life.*
>
> *In love, light, and gratitude,"*

So my hope for you is that these *5 Keys To Turning Adversities Into Allies* have helped you recognize that you have everything you need right now to overcome any adversity in your life, and hopefully they will encourage you to create an attitude of gratitude that allows you to be grateful for this amazing gift called *life*.

Good luck!

"You are more than your thoughts, your body, or your feelings. You are a swirling vortex of limitless potential who is here to shake things up and create something new that the Universe has never seen."

Dr. Richard Bartlett

Chapter 2
Who Are You?

I would like for you to take a moment to reread below the quote from the previous page.

> *"You are more than your thoughts, your body, or your feelings. You are a swirling vortex of limitless potential who is here to shake things up and create something new that the Universe has never seen."*

As you read the quote, what thoughts came to mind? How did you feel after reading it? Did you feel excited? Scared? Confused? Uncertain? What if the quote is true? What if I told you that you are an unlimited being with infinite potential?

Would you believe me?

Unfortunately, most people wouldn't. But the fact that you are reading this book right now tells me that you are not "most people". If you are the type of person who reads a book like this, that tells me that you are open minded, curious, and willing to learn and grow, and therefore it's quite possible that you believe the quote. As a matter of fact, you've probably already agreed with it and are now ready to create something new that the Universe has never seen - so let's just jump right in and get started.

The truth is, there's an overwhelming majority of people who do not believe the quote. They will accept societally-driven labels that define who they are without ever asking themselves deeper questions like "who am I and why am I here?" This chapter is designed to give you some insights on possibly answering those two questions for you. Are you ready to answer those questions for yourself?

If you ask most people who they are, they will usually respond with answers such as their name, whether they have a family, what they do for a living, if they are a democrat or republican, an African American or Caucasian, a Christian or a Muslim (or are part of a host of other religions), an American or Asian - the list of labels goes on and on. But if you think really deeply about this, these are just titles and labels that we use to try to define who we are. To prove my point, I want you to do a simple test. Walk up to a mirror and ask yourself what you see. Do you see a republican? A Christian? A husband? A manager?

The answer is that you see a human being. The mirror can't lie, it can only reflect that which is placed in front of it. All the titles and labels that you use to define yourself isn't who you are; they are simply titles, labels, and beliefs that you have accepted to define yourself. For example, have you ever known someone who used to be a republican, but then became a democrat? Or someone who was a Christian, who then became a Muslim? Or maybe someone who was pro-life, then became pro-choice? If they looked in the mirror as a republican and then became a democrat what would they see in the mirror? They would see a human being, not a label. Labels are really just beliefs. You are not a label. You are a human being with different beliefs, and although your beliefs may change, you will not.

What you see in the mirror is what you truly are, but it goes a lot deeper than that. *What* you are, is not necessarily *who* you are.

Let me explain in more detail.

What you are is a human being with flesh and bones. This is an undisputable fact. But *who* you are is the divine being that resides within the flesh and bones. Here is another way to look at it - if I stand in front of a mirror and look at myself, I notice that I'm wearing a shirt. So if I say that is "my" shirt, who owns it? I do - it is "my" shirt. Now, I continue to look into the mirror and notice my body. Who is the "me" that owns the body? If this is "my" body, who am I? I would like to suggest that the "me" that owns the body is actually my spirit. Put another way, you are not actually a human being having a spiritual experience - you are a spiritual being having a human experience, and your body is just like the suit of clothes that you are wearing.

If you can wrap your mind around this idea then the original quote that I began this chapter with should make more sense to you. The quote said "You are a swirling vortex of limitless potential who is here to shake things up and create something new that the Universe has never seen." Which simply means that you are a divine spiritual being expressing yourself through human form. You have unique gifts and talents that must be shared with the world if you truly want to live a rewarding and fulfilling life.

So what do you think? Do you believe this? Can you accept that you are much more than your physical body? Can you embrace the idea that you are a divine spiritual being with unlimited potential who is here to shake things up?

Since you're still reading this book that means you're

ready to dive deep into who you really are! So let's begin with understanding your divine makeup.

You are actually a three part being which can be described as body, mind, and spirit. You are a spirit, which is housed in a body that has a mind. Your body is like the clothes you are wearing, and your mind is like a tool that you use to help make conscious decisions and to learn new things. They all work in harmony.

As a spiritual being, you have an infinite capacity for learning and creativity. There are absolutely no limits to the amount of things you can learn and create. You are only limited by your imagination, and even your imagination is unlimited.

So, let's break down the three parts of your being.

Let's begin with your mind.

It's important that you understand what your mind is and how it works if you truly want to discover who you really are. I'll begin by saying that the mind and the brain are not really the same thing. Your brain is the organ that serves as the center of your nervous system and is responsible for cognitive thinking and memory. In my opinion, it is the most amazing organ in your body, and it works just like a muscle - the more you use it, the stronger it gets.

The mind, however, is separate and distinct from the brain, although they work together. It is almost impossible to truly define the mind. Scientists have been trying to define it in scientific terms for millennia, but unfortunately there has never been a consensus on exactly what the mind is. Rather than try to argue and define it, I will simply share a definition that I truly resonate with, and it is this definition I will use to explain what I believe the mind does and how it works.

The mind is *"the element of a person that enables them to be aware of the world and their experiences, to think, and to feel; the faculty of consciousness and thought."*

I really like the last part of this definition; *the faculty of consciousness and thought.*

According to Dr. Bruce Lipton, author of the amazing book The Biology Of Belief, the mind actually has two parts; the conscious mind and the subconscious mind. A great metaphor to explain how it works is an iceberg. If you look at an iceberg in the ocean you will only see a small portion of it above the water, but did you know that in some cases 90% of the iceberg is actually below the surface? This is how the mind works. The top 10% is your conscious mind, and the lower 90% is your subconscious mind. What is really fascinating is that the subconscious mind is actually 1000 times more powerful than the conscious mind when it comes to influencing your behavior.

Dr. Lipton explained it this way;

> *When we are born, we are completely conscious of all the external stimuli that we interact with. As children we process primarily through our feelings without judgment or thought about the situation. In other words, we use our hearts, not our minds, to interpret everything around us. Our feelings become the guidepost of our experiences.*
>
> *During the first 7-10 years of our lives, our*

subconscious mind works like a video recorder. It simply records all the external events in our lives, and then it begins associating feelings, memories, and beliefs with those events. As we grow older, we begin to form subconscious beliefs about everything we come into contact with. As we form these beliefs we then begin making assumptions about who we are and how we fit into the world. Our prerecorded tapes become our subconscious beliefs about ourselves, and everything we think and do are then filtered through, and influenced by, these prerecorded tapes.

So take a moment to think about your own childhood, especially between when you were born and when you turned seven. What do you remember? Do you remember growing up in a loving, caring home, or was it one filled with violence and dysfunction?

Whether you realize it or not, your childhood has a strong impact on your behavior, even as an adult. If you remember being loved and nurtured as a child, the chances are your subconscious mind is filled with positive beliefs about yourself. In other words, your prerecorded tapes are positive, which in most cases means you will feel good about yourself and have a positive attitude about life. On the other hand, if you remember pain and misery growing up, there is a good chance that your prerecorded tapes about yourself may be negative, which in turn may cause you to create a negative outlook on life.

You can look at the subconscious mind as a big memory bank that stores your beliefs, memories, and life experiences. All your thoughts are instantly processed through your subconscious beliefs. Look at it this way - once your subconscious tapes are programmed during your childhood, every thought and action you have as an adult will be based on the programming you experienced growing up.

I'd like to take this time to share an example from my own life.

I was separated from my mom at the age of six, where I then created a subconscious belief that the people who love you will always leave you. As an adult that may sound irrational, but as a six-year-old, my mother meant the world to me and having her leave me was devastating and emotionally traumatizing.

As a result of this event, I created a subconscious belief that there was something wrong with me that caused my mother to leave. The primary belief I created was that I was unlovable. In order not to feel the shame and abandonment I experienced when my mother left, I created an unconscious strategy that I thought would keep me from feeling pain, and also to keep people in my life from leaving.

That strategy was for me to become a super nice guy in hopes of keeping people around that I cared about. By becoming a super nice guy I put other people's emotional and psychological needs ahead of my own, and I was constantly trying to take care of others before taking care of myself. This is called *co-dependence*, and it was the reason I struggled with relationships earlier in my life.

I didn't realize it as I was growing up, but that single event laid the foundation of how I interacted in all of my relationships as an adult. My subconscious beliefs about myself actually sabotaged my relationships.

I would enter into a relationship where I would be the super nice guy. I would do all the right things that a woman would want in a relationship. I was attentive and respectful, and I had no problems showing affection. I had a great sense of humor and definitely believed in monogamy. On the surface I appeared to be the perfect guy, but unfortunately my subconscious beliefs about not being good enough and the deep-seated fear of abandonment kept me from being truly authentic in relationships, which kept me from experiencing true intimacy. No matter how much a woman loved me, that deep-rooted fear I had convinced me that something was wrong with me, which led to the fear that eventually the women in my life would leave.

Based on this subconscious fear, what do you think happened in my relationships? Of course, the women in my life would leave. I created an amazing pattern in all of my relationships, especially after my divorce. I would enter into a relationship and it would last two to three weeks, and then the women would end up saying that they "cared too much" about me to stay in the relationship.

At the time, it made absolutely no sense to me that women would say that. How could you care about someone, but at the same time leave them? After some deep self-introspection and emotional healing, I was able to recognize how my subconscious beliefs had been sabotaging my relationships, and I figured out how to break the pattern (I will explain how I did this in the next chapter).

The point I'm trying to make is how powerful the subconscious mind really is. Remember, the subconscious mind is separate and distinct from your brain - it is the faculty of consciousness and thought.

On the other hand, you have your conscious mind, which could be referred to as your "intellect". The conscious mind is where you store information that you have learned through rigorous study and learning. When you go to school and learn facts, you are using your conscious mind. When you calculate and figure out solutions to most problems, you are also using your conscious mind, but remember what I said about the subconscious mind being 1000 times more powerful than the conscious mind?

Here is an example of how this works.

Imagine that you know someone that has a PhD in astrophysics. This person is obviously extremely intelligent, and has a highly-developed conscious mind. But imagine too that this person has difficulty creating healthy relationships. No matter what they do, they always experience difficulty in relationships. Why do you think this is? They are obviously very smart, and yet they can't figure out how to make relationships work. Why is that?

Well, it's actually pretty simple. On a conscious level they can read a book about relationships and explain to you intellectually how relationships work, which uses the conscious mind. But their subconscious is 1000 times more powerful than their conscious mind, so when they enter into a relationship, the subconscious beliefs they have about themselves will always override the conscious mind. No matter how many books they read or how smart they are, if they have deeply rooted negative subconscious beliefs about themselves, they will never be able to create healthy relationships.

This is why it is so important to understand how the mind works. No matter how much we may learn on a conscious level, if we aren't willing to look at our subconscious beliefs, we can never truly change our lives. We each have deeply held subconscious beliefs about a wide variety of things and until we become willing to change these subconscious beliefs, we will not be able to overcome our subconscious conditioning.

Let's take a look at some subconscious beliefs that may be sabotaging your life right now.

Are you currently struggling financially and can't figure out why? Well, there is a very good chance that your subconscious beliefs are actually keeping you from being financially secure. If you grew up hearing that money was the root of all evil or that rich people were stuck up and selfish, you may have subconscious beliefs that keep you from making a lot of money, because your subconscious belief might be that money is "bad".

If you're a man and you struggle with relationships, you may have subconscious beliefs that say women only want you for your money or women can't be trusted. This belief will eventually sabotage any new relationship you enter. If you're a woman and struggle with relationships, then it's quite possible that you have subconscious beliefs that say all men are dogs and only want sex. Therefore this belief will keep you from creating true intimacy with men because of your lack of trust. If you happen to be religious, you may have subconscious beliefs that you are a sinner and there is nothing you can do except repent of your sins and hope that God forgives you for being a sinner.

No matter what subconscious beliefs you have, you must understand that it is those subconscious beliefs that are actually the cause of most of the pain, suffering, and lack of experience you have in life. To sum it up, your subconscious beliefs create your reality, so if you aren't happy with any area of your life right now, I can assure you that the main reason is that you have some unconscious belief that is causing you pain and misery.

It is absolutely imperative that you begin examining your deeply held subconscious beliefs if you truly want to change, but rest assured that it *is* possible for you to do so.

Now that you have a deeper understanding of how the subconscious mind works, here's the really good news - when you realize just how powerful the mind really is, you can use it to create anything you want in life.

Have you ever heard this quote: "Whatever the mind can conceive, you can achieve, if you really believe"?

Do you believe it? Is it really possible?

I believe the answer is "yes" and now I would like to share how and why this is possible. So let's go back to the definition I posted earlier: The mind is *"the element of a person that enables them to be aware of the world and their experiences, to think, and to feel; the faculty of consciousness and thought."*

I would like you to focus on *"the faculty of consciousness and thought."*

Here is another way to look at it. Try to imagine there is a Divine Intelligence that permeates the Universe. This Intelligence is actually the Source of all things. It is inherent in all things. It is what keeps the planets aligned and what causes a seed to grow into a flower. It is the same intelligence that causes a bone to heal and the earth to orbit the sun.

There are lots of different names for this Source, but the name does not matter. You can call it God, The Creator, Yahweh, Jehovah, Great Spirit, The Universe, or any other name, but what is most important is that you believe and trust that it is available to you (throughout this book I will simply refer to it as The Source). You do not have to believe in any particular religion or dogma to have access to it, you must simply open your heart and your mind to the truth that it exists. If you accept this truth, then you must accept that your mind is actually connected to The Source. Your mind is like a conduit through which The Source allows divine intelligence to flow to you and through you.

Now you must remember what I said at the beginning. **The mind and the brain are not the same thing.** The brain can only process information that you have provided to it. The brain is not creative - it is not the source of imagination, creativity, or divine ideas. The brain is also not the source of inspiration or insight; these are all functions of the mind, which can also be referred to as the heart, or the center of your being.

Author and spiritual teacher Iyanla Vanzant said *"The*

mind is a powerful, creative energy. Everything we think, do, and feel begins in the mind. For this reason, we have to address the thoughts, beliefs, judgments, learning's, and perceptions that we hold in our minds."

The reason the quote "whatever the mind can conceive you can achieve" is true, is because The Source of all things is purely creative and it needs you to co-create with it. So when your mind conceives a divine idea from The Source, which is all-powerful and limitless, you can accomplish it if you're willing to work hand-in-hand with The Source and put forth a whole lot of effort to bring it to fruition.

One of my favorite spiritual teachers is Deepak Chopra. He shared a very powerful quote that really speaks to this truth. He said: "Inherent in every intention and desire are the mechanics for its fulfillment". Put another way, The Source will not give you an idea that you can't accomplish. The Source knows exactly what you're capable of, and will therefore only give you divine ideas that are attainable for you. You wouldn't even have the idea in the first place if you weren't capable of accomplishing it.

As I mentioned previously, the mind is the source of imagination, and therefore it is the key to creating anything you want in life. Let me share a brief story with you to validate my point.

During the darkest period of my life I was deeply depressed and unsure of how I was ever going to get my life back on track. At the time, I had no money, no job, no relationship, no material possessions, and things seemed pretty hopeless. But the one thing I did have was my imagination, and I began to use it to help me change my situation. Despite that I had absolutely nothing, I began imagining my life getting better. Instead of focusing on all the things I didn't have, I focused my attention on what I did have. I would begin each day counting my blessings for everything that I had, such as my health, my ability to learn, my positive attitude, a few close friends, children who loved me, and the fact that I was even alive.

I began envisioning what my life would be like once I got back on my feet, and I somehow knew that eventually I would. As I continued to focus on the things that I did have and on the future that I wanted to create, things slowly started to change for me. Eventually I found a job, then I purchased a car, and finally I was able to get my own apartment. Although this took a couple of years, my point is that I used my imagination to see the things I wanted, and then I worked really hard to get them. It all began in my mind. I had to be willing to use my mind and imagination first before I could create the things I wanted.

As I think back in retrospect I can now see how The Source was actually the source of all of the ideas that I used to put my life back together. It was The Source that would provide me with ideas on where to look for employment, and that gave me the inspiration to remain positive even when I had nothing. It was The Source that gave me the strength and courage to move through all of my life's challenges without giving up and falling victim to despair. It was The Source that encouraged me and helped me to focus on my ultimate destiny, and it didn't allow me to quit.

Even through those difficult times, I held on to my dreams of one day being a successful entrepreneur, writer, and speaker. I had no evidence that I could do these things, I only had the belief and faith that I could. Belief and faith originate in the mind, and I now recognize that each of these originate from The Source.

And now here I am, some twenty years later doing exactly what I imagined I would be doing. All because I chose to believe that whatever the mind can conceive, you can achieve.

It's important that you understand I am no different than you are. I am a divine spiritual being with direct access to The Source, and so are you. You have a mind and direct access to The Source. There is nothing you cannot accomplish if you choose to access your divinity, but it is up to you to go a little deeper and figure out what negative subconscious beliefs you may have about yourself and change them. It is your responsibility to learn more about your mind and begin using it to create the life you deserve. This is simply an overview of how your mind works. I will share more insights in the upcoming chapter titled Intuition/Synchronicity, but for now, I simply want you to accept and understand that your mind is the most important aspect of your humanity. Don't take it for granted. Use it to create the life you were born to live. It is your greatest gift from The Source.

So, now let's talk about your body.

It is my belief that the most amazing thing on this planet is the human body. I do not believe that there is anything more miraculous. Although most people take their bodies for granted, I believe it is the greatest gift that The Source provided us with. I mentioned earlier that the body is simply a suit of clothing that your spirit wears, so I must admit that The Source knew exactly what it was doing when it created the human body.

Of course, everyone is aware of their own physical body, but did you know that you also have an emotional or energetic body?

If you accept the fact that you are a spiritual being, then it makes it easier to grasp how the emotional/energetic body works.

Think of it this way;

Imagine that you have an opening in the top of your skull, and there is a pipe that goes from the top of your skull to the bottom of your belly. This pipe flows with energy that comes directly from The Source; this energy is your life force, and it permeates your entire being. When you are born, the pipe is completely open and it allows Source energy to flow through you easily. This energy causes you to feel alive and connected to life. This energy is then converted into feelings, which is the spirit's way of communicating with the body. There are primarily four energies that move throughout the energetic body; joy, anger, sadness, and fear.

As a child, whenever you experienced one of these feelings you acted appropriately and expressed the feeling through an emotion. For example, if you felt sad you would cry; if you felt angry you would scream or lash out; if you felt joy you would smile and laugh; and if you felt fear you would close off or retreat. As long as you expressed the feeling appropriately, then the energetic pipe stayed open and clear and your life force energy continues to flow through you.

As you grow older, your parents or family members begin conditioning you to believe that expressing them was wrong, so what happens is you begin to repress and suppress your feelings, and each time you do you begin to create little energy blocks in the pipe. It's like building up plaque in your arteries. The more you suppress your feelings, the more the energetic pipe clogs up, and before you know it the pipe is completely closed and you are cut off from your life force. When this happens you lose your sense of aliveness, because the divine flow of energy has been cut off. Once the flow of energy has been cut off and we have been disconnected from The Source, we then learn to process everything through our conscious mind or intellect, and we become very rational and analytical. In other words, we try to rely on our brains instead of our minds and hearts.

The bad news is the energetic body works like the subconscious mind. We may not be aware of it, but our repressed emotions cause us to act out irrationally sometimes because we are completely unconscious of the pain we may be carrying. Here is a good example. Have you ever met someone or known someone who is always angry? No matter what is going, on this person is angry and negative, and they usually aren't that pleasant to be around. They get angry and upset at the slightest provocation, and no matter what you say or do they will have a negative response to just about everything. Do you know anyone like that? Are *you* like that?

Why do you think this person acts this way? It's because

they have trapped emotional energy in their emotional body, and until they learn how to release it, they will always act out of anger.

On the flip side of that, maybe you know someone who always pretends to be happy. They are the "people pleasing" types that always seek approval and they pretend that everything is always okay. The only emotion they express is happiness, but unfortunately they are completely sad and emotionally bankrupt inside. A person like this usually has trapped anger, fear, or sadness in their emotional bodies, and rather than feel these emotions they hide behind being happy all of the time.

When we have repressed or suppressed emotions they can sabotage all areas of our lives. As long as we feel and release our feelings appropriately, the life force can move through us, but as we shut down the flow, we create a disconnection from The Source and it leads to all sorts of problems in our lives.

It's important that you take care of both of your bodies - your physical body and your emotional one. You take care of the physical body by eating the right foods and exercising, and you take care of the emotional body by investing in some emotional healing work that allows you to release any repressed energy that is trapped in your emotional body. I will share some tips on how to do this in the next chapter.

Now that you have a better understanding of how the mind and the body works together, it's time to fully understand who you really are.

Every major religion promotes a very simple and

profound truth. There is a Source through which all things are created. It does not matter which religion you follow, as long as you accept this simple fact. This Source is the Divine Intelligence that created and is still creating the Universe, and you have unlimited access to this Source. As a human being you are a divine expression of this Source, which means that you can co-create anything your heart desires with this Source.

Think of it this way - if you look at the ocean, you will see a powerful, beautiful, and seemingly infinite body of water. If you walk up to the ocean and scoop up a small cup of it, what you will have in the cup is ocean. But the cup of ocean could never be the ocean in its totality, so therefore it is a divine expression of the ocean. This expression is no different than the ocean; as a matter of fact it contains all of the same qualities, characteristics, and attributes of the ocean. In fact, it is the ocean in an individualized expression. As long as the expression of the ocean stays connected to the ocean it will thrive and express exactly the way the ocean does. But if the ocean in the cup is separated from the ocean, eventually it will dry up and no longer exist as that unique expression.

The Source is just like the ocean. You are an individual expression of the Source. You have all of the same qualities, characteristics, and attributes as the Source. You are no different than The Source. As long as you stay connected to The Source, you can co-create with it, and since The Source is infinite, so are you.

Do not buy into societal labels and constructs that will convince you that there is something wrong with you. Disregard all labels and titles and come to the understanding that you are a divine spiritual being with unlimited potential, and the only thing that can keep you from accomplishing anything is yourself. This includes letting go of your attachment of your ethnic identity. You should definitely be proud of your ethnic heritage, whatever it may be, but you must understand that your spiritual nature has nothing to do with skin color or nationality. The Source transcends race, and therefore so do you if you choose to accept who and what you truly are.

Titles and labels will only hold you back, but accepting the truth of your being will definitely set you free. Remember that you are a three part being - Spirit, Mind, and Body - that is connected to The Source, and you can therefore co-create anything your heart desires.

I would like to close this chapter with something for you to think about.

I would like for you to think about a snowflake.

If you look at snowflakes falling from the sky, it appears that they are all the same. They all have the same color, texture, and smell. They are all composed of the same stuff, and they all come from the same source. But if you look under a microscope, every snowflake is completely different. No two snowflakes are alike. Just imagine – out of the billions of snowflakes that fall from the sky, none of them are the same.

The truth is, you are just like the snowflake. Out of the 7 billion human beings on the planet, there is only one you. When it comes to human beings, The Source never replicates itself. You are a divine, unique individual expression of The Source, and it is your responsibility to accept this fact.

Your job is to come to this understanding and to recognize that you have unlimited potential, and you have been given some unique gifts and talents that are yours alone - and your job is to share them with the world. This is the reason that the quote I shared at the beginning of chapter is so important. It states a divine truth, and I hope that you will take it to heart and accept it as *your* truth.

So I will leave you with that quote, and I hope that you will embrace it and accept the truth that it shares.

> *"You are more than your thoughts, your body, or your feelings. You are a swirling vortex of limitless potential who is here to shake things up and create something new that the Universe has never seen."*
>
> **Dr. Richard Bartlett**

Whatever the mind can conceive, you can achieve, if you truly believe.

Conceive it!

Believe it!

Achieve it!

"There is no coming to consciousness without pain. People will do anything, no matter how absurd, in order to avoid facing their own soul. One does not become enlightened by imagining figures of light, but by making the darkness conscious."

Carl G. Jung

Chapter 3
Make Peace With Your Past

When I became involved with personal development programs back in 1990 I was really drawn in to the teaching of the power of positive thinking. I had always been an optimistic person, so it was a natural progression for me to really embrace what a lot of the motivational speakers were preaching. Their message was to always be positive and look at the bright side of things. It was this positive thinking that allowed me to deal with the multiplicity of challenges I was dealing with at the time. If not for my positive thinking, I'm sure that I would have fallen into a deep abyss of despair and depression, which may have ultimately ended up with my demise.

But I embraced the positive thinking mantra and made a commitment to always think positive. Without question, this way of thinking has positively impacted my life, but there was a negative side of positive thinking that I want to share, to shed some light on why positive thinking sometimes doesn't work and can also be detrimental to your life.

The biggest lesson I learned about the detrimental effects of positive thinking occurred while I was basically homeless. I had a friend that allowed me to stay at her house for a while until I could find a place of my own. During that time I was searching for employment and doing everything I could to get back on my feet. I didn't own a car and she would sometimes let me borrow hers to look for employment. She was an absolute angel whom I am forever indebted to for her generosity, caring, and friendship.

One evening my friend came home and asked me how my day went. I told her about the rejections I had received while trying to find a job, and I told her that I was still optimistic that I would find a job soon.

She then looked at me with a caring compassionate heart and she asked how I was really doing. The conversation went something like this:

> Her: *Michael, tell me how you're really doing. How are you feeling right now?*
>
> Me: *I'm doing great! Although I didn't find a job I'm confident that I will soon and I will be able to get back on my feet.*
>
> Her: *But Michael, you didn't answer my question. How are you feeling right now? In this very moment how do you feel?*
>
> Me: *I told you I'm doing great. I know the Universe is going to support me and help me find a job so I'm excited and happy about my future.*
>
> Her: *Michael, I think that's bullshit! You keep saying you're doing great but the truth is you aren't. Right now your life is a mess and you're unwilling to be completely honest with yourself about how you really feel. I believe in you and have faith in you that you will get your life on track, but until you are able to be completely honest with yourself about how you feel, not what you think, you really won't be able to change. I personally think that you are in denial and you are hiding behind your positive thinking and denying how you really feel. Can you tell me right now exactly what you're feeling?*

Me: *I told you, I'm doing great. I've got some challenges to deal with but I keep telling you that I'll deal with them. What more do you want me to say?*

Her: *I want you to share your feelings with me. Tell me what's going on inside you. Not what's in your head, but what's in your heart. How do you feel?*

Me: *I don't really understand what you're asking. I keep telling you that I'm fine. What else can I say?*

Her: *So Michael, answer this question, how does it make you feel to not be able to have your own home and have to rely on other people? Does it make you sad? Does it make you angry?*

How did you feel when you were rejected for the jobs you applied for today? Were you upset? Were you disappointed? Were you afraid?

Or how does it make you feel when you know you can't see your kids because you don't have transportation or money to visit them? Doesn't that make you feel sad?

Do you see what I mean now? I want you to share your emotions with me. I want you to express your feelings. Can you do that?

Me: *I'm not sure.*

Her: *Michael, you and I have been through a lot together as friends. I love how you are able to be optimistic and positive, and I love how you can find the good in all situations. But the truth is you aren't connected to your emotions and you hide behind* being positive and intellectual. You are so stuck in your head that you can't feel from your heart.

You are my friend and I love you. I will never judge you or reject you. I'm not asking anything from you except your willingness to be authentic and real with me. Can you do that? Can you share yourself with me in that way?

After listening to her for a moment I started to allow myself to feel. I really started looking closer at myself for what emotions were present, and all of a sudden I knew what she meant. In that moment I felt my heart beginning to surrender and I began to speak.

Me*: I understand what you mean now. If I'm completely honest I feel sad and afraid. I'm sad because I feel like less than a man because I have to rely on you to take care of me. I feel afraid that I'm not going to be able to find a job and ultimately you will have to kick me out on the streets and I'm not sure what I will do.*

Her: *That's what I'm talking about. Keep sharing. Tell me more about how you feel.*

Me: *I really feel like a failure right now. I worked so hard to build my perfect life, only to have it come crashing down on me. I've lost everything. I lost my wife, my kids, my home, my job, and my self-esteem. I feel lonely and sad right now.*

All of a sudden my friend walks over and begins to hug me. She takes me in her arms and tells me that everything is going to be okay. She assures me that it is okay to share what I'm feeling, and that it does not make me less of a man to do so. As she continued to hold me in her warm embrace, I continued to share how I was feeling. I allowed all the trapped emotions to come out and the tears began to flow. I found myself releasing years of repressed pain, sadness, and disappointment, and the emotions just began to pour out of me through my tears. Although it was extremely painful, it was also therapeutic. Allowing myself to feel and express those emotions was extremely healing and cathartic. Before long my tears of sadness and pain turned to tears of joy, as I recognized just how much my friend cared about me and how much love I was feeling from her in that moment.

> Me: *I am so glad we are having this conversation because I'm really tired of pretending that everything is okay. I have been hiding behind this new-age spiritual positive thinking mask for so long I haven't allowed myself just to feel my emotions. I guess there was a part of me that believed if I shared the negative things in my life it meant that I didn't have faith that it would get better. But now I realize this isn't true. Just because I may be feeling sad or afraid does not mean that I've lost faith, it just means that I'm human and I have feelings and I should always be aware of, and true to, those feelings.*

> Her: *The key to happiness is being in touch with how you truly feel and being able to express whatever you feel openly and honestly. Feelings are neither good nor bad, they just are. Emotions are just energy in motion which really is a human being's way of receiving internal feedback and then expressing*

your internal response to external stimuli. In reality, our emotions are our internal guidance system that keeps us in touch with our humanness.

Now that we've had this conversation, I hope that you will be able to speak with me openly and honestly about how you really feel, and you should know that negativity isn't necessarily a bad thing. If you focus on it too much it can make matters worse, but the key is to always be honest with how you really feel, no matter what situation you may be in. I accept you unconditionally as a friend and I'm going to be here for you even when things are tough. You don't have to impress me with your optimism and intellect because I accept you for who you are, not what you do. Do you understand?

Me: *I really do. This experience has really been good for me and it has opened my eyes to the fact that I still have some healing and some growing to do. Thank you so much for seeing through my positive mask and challenging me to take it off. I promise that I will do my best to be as open and as honest as I possibly can when I'm speaking with you. Thank you so much for being my friend. I love you!*

After that conversation I had to carry out some deep soul searching to figure out exactly why it was so difficult for me to initially express my feelings to my friend. As I contemplated our conversation I was able to see a pattern in my life that I had been using for a very long time. I always used positivity as a way of not expressing my true feelings to others, and I always sought other people's approval to feel good about myself.

I knew that I wanted to break this pattern, and I decided that I would figure out what steps I needed to take to do so.

I decided to talk to my friend to see if she could begin shedding some light on my behavior. She informed me that one of the reasons why I may have had so much difficulty expressing my feelings could have been the result of some childhood trauma. She shared her own experience about going to therapy to deal with some issues from her childhood, and she suggested that I consider therapy that may help me deal with my issues.

She then said something that really stood out for me. It was a statement that was so powerful it literally caused me to rethink everything I had learned in the personal development arena. She looked at me and said; "I don't care how positive you are, how many books you read, or how many seminars you go to. Until you make peace with your past you will never truly be happy."

It was this statement that challenged me to thoroughly examine my entire philosophy on personal development.

I then realized that all the motivational seminars and books I had read did not help me make peace with my past, so I decided to make it the number one priority in my life. I intuitively knew that making peace with my past was the missing link to finding true happiness.

I recently ran across a quote by author and spiritual teacher Iyanla Vanzant that fully embodies why making peace with your past is so important. This powerful quote holds the key to your happiness and I suggest that you read it slowly (and several times) and intently so that you fully grasp the implications of its message.

> *"Until you heal the wounds of your past, you are going to bleed. You can bandage the bleeding with food, with alcohol, with drugs, with work, with cigarettes, with sex; but eventually, it will all ooze through and stain your life. You must find the strength to open the wounds, stick your hands inside, pull out the core of the pain that is holding you in your past, the memories, and make peace with them."*

Herein lies the key to your happiness. What I've learned over the last twenty years is that we must be willing to heal our hearts and make peace with our past if we truly want to be happy. We can read all the self-help books in the world and listen to audio programs or go to seminars with motivational speakers, but if we fail to carry out our healing work we will unconsciously sabotage our lives and ultimately keep ourselves from being completely happy.

Amazingly there are some people who do not believe that their childhood can actually have an adverse effect on their adult lives. Have you ever heard someone say that their parents used to beat them when they were little, yet they still turned out okay? This statement is a defense mechanism that keeps people trapped in their pain and they will rationalize that their traumatic childhoods had no effect on them whatsoever. The truth is, if you remember being beaten as a child and you have not done any healing work, I can assure you that it will have an effect on your life today.

If you read the preceding chapter and the part about the subconscious mind, this should make sense to you. There are negative beliefs that you may have stored about yourself that could be causing you to unconsciously sabotage your life. This can show up as failed relationships, anxiety, depression, anger issues, or an overall feeling that something is simply missing from your life.

The key to making peace with your past lies in your willingness to heal any emotional scars that you may be carrying from your childhood. Healing your heart is the key to making peace with your past. Psychologists will tell you that at their core, all addictions have an unresolved emotional conflict, which simply means that there are **emotional wounds that need to be healed.**

What Iyanla Vanzant meant when she said *"You must find the strength to open the wounds, stick your hands inside, pull out the core of the pain that is holding you in your past, the memories, and make peace with them"* is that it is your responsibility to look within your own heart and find where the pain is, and be willing to heal that pain.

There is a powerful scene in the movie Star Wars, in which Luke Skywalker is being trained by the Master Teacher Yoda. In the scene, Yoda tells Luke that he must enter into a dark cave to face his demons and ultimately become a Jedi Knight. As Luke begins to look into the cave, he turns to Yoda and asks: "What's in the cave." To which Yoda replies; "Only what you take with you." As Luke goes into the cave he is confronted by his nemesis, Darth Vader. Darth Vader is the antagonist in the movie who embraces "The Dark Side." As Darth Vader approaches, Luke pulls out his Light Saber and begins fighting with him. After a brief battle, Luke chops off Darth Vader's head and it appears that he has defeated the bad guy. As Luke looks at the severed head, smoke suddenly issues from the helmet Vader is wearing. As the smoke clears, Luke looks inside the helmet and sees his own face.

The symbolism of this scene speaks directly to the importance of making peace with your past. Luke Skywalker represents the good in every human being, and his training with the Master represents the importance of having teachers to guide us on our personal growth journeys to find the good that is within us. The dark cave represents your subconscious mind that stores all of your erroneous negative beliefs about yourself. It is the place where fear resides, and we must be willing to enter the cave if we truly want to make peace with our past and not live in fear.

Darth Vader represents the parts of ourselves that we are sometimes afraid to look at. He symbolizes our shadows, which are the parts of ourselves that we sometimes hide, suppress, or deny. The battle represents the struggle that we must go through in order to shed light on the dark places in our minds and hearts that keep us from expressing who we really are. Cutting off Darth Vader's head and then Luke seeing his own face represents facing our demons within, and then allowing the dark parts of ourselves to die so that we can be resurrected into who we truly are.

The key is to remember what Yoda said about what's in the cave. "Only what you take with you." This means that the darkness we perceive is only in our minds. The so called darkness is simply erroneous beliefs that we hold about ourselves, and when we become courageous enough to face our own inner darkness, that part of us dies and the real part of us awakens.

There are some people who prescribe to the idea that you do not have to address your childhood wounds in order to be successful and happy. They believe that it does not do any good to "dig up" old hurts. I completely disagree with this way of thinking. I believe that it is absolutely imperative that you are willing to look at the dark events in your life, and are willing to shed light on them. If you are unwilling to do so, those dark places will eventually sabotage your happiness.

There is a term called "spiritual bypassing", which means a person refuses to heal their inner wounds because they have accepted a specific religious teaching that says that God can heal you. I used to hold that belief. At one time I thought that if I prayed enough and followed religious dogma and doctrine, then I would eventually become happy. My own experience has taught me otherwise. It wasn't until I became courageous enough to make peace with my past and deal with some childhood trauma that I was able to heal my heart and become genuinely happy.

When I decided that I wanted to heal my wounds I was introduced to a man named John Bradshaw who facilitated a program called Healing Your Inner Child. In one of his workshops I learned how my abusive childhood was at the core of all the dysfunction in my life. I learned that I had abandonment issues as a result of being separated from my mom when I was six years old, and I also learned that for the majority of my adult life I was driven by a deep sense of shame. It was my internal feelings of shame that drove me to be successful. I worked really hard to gain other people's approval because deep down I didn't feel worthy.

Although it was extremely difficult, I made the choice to heal my heart and make peace with my past. I took Iyanla's advice and found the strength to open my wounds and stick my hands inside and pull out the core of my pain that was keeping me trapped in my past - and I made peace with them.

As a result of doing this work, I can honestly admit in this very moment I am happier today than I've ever been in my life. It definitely wasn't easy, but I can assure you that it was worth it.

I hope that you will take some time and really think about what I've just shared. Do not make the same mistakes that I did in thinking that being positive will solve all of your problems. Of course there is absolutely nothing wrong with being positive, and I am still a huge advocate of positive thinking. The key is to make sure that you aren't hiding behind positivity because of some unresolved emotional pain the way I did.

If you are committed to making peace with your past and are looking for some ways to do so, let me make a few suggestions for you to consider. First of all, I think it's really important that you are willing to seek support if needed. I realize that there is a lot of negative stigma attached in seeking support, but that is a sign of strength, not weakness, when you choose to seek help.

Here are a few things for you to consider if you are truly ready to make peace with your past.

1. Therapy

There is nothing wrong with seeking out a good therapist to support you in dealing with any emotional challenges you may be facing. Our society has conditioned us to believe that we are supposed to carry the weight of the world on our shoulders and not seek support, but this simply isn't true. We all need support at one time or another, so if you've been looking for ways to help you make peace with your past, a good therapist may be exactly what you need.

I would like to share an article I wrote a while ago that shares my first experience with therapy. My hope is that it will give you some insight on how difficult and challenging it might be, but also to inspire you to take the first step if you think you will benefit from therapy. The article is titled "Men's Emotional Healing."

In 1989 I had a series of traumatic experiences that were beginning to take their toll. My divorce and separation from my kids were extremely painful and had begun to negatively impact my life. I had slipped into a deep state of depression and was barely able to function on a daily basis. As my depression deepened I went into isolation, where I literally shut myself off from the outside world.

Although I was able to go to work and function in that capacity, I was completely disconnected from any social settings. I was not dating, and I did not socialize with my friends. I also had difficulty sleeping. I would rarely eat and I had begun to lose weight, which was rare for me, being a former personal trainer that took excellent care of my physical body. After several months I began to have fleeting thoughts of suicide, and it appeared that my situation was hopeless. In an effort to alleviate some of the pain, I begin to read books dealing with depression.

As I read them I could see myself in some of the stories. I definitely had all of the symptoms of depression, and I knew that I had to deal with it head on if I ever wanted to get my life back on track. After reading several books I realized that I was still deeply depressed and had not really begun to deal with the issues that were causing my depression. Instinctively I knew that I needed help, and I decided that I would seek therapy.

After making the decision to get help, another series of challenges surfaced. First of all, how was I going to find a therapist? How would I know which one to choose? What if the therapist couldn't help me? Would I be able to change? Could therapy "fix" me? What about the money to pay for it? I was completely broke and definitely couldn't pay someone to listen to my problems. What was I going to do? These were just a few of the questions that were going through my mind.

 My greatest fear was wondering what would happen if my employees found out. As a manager, I was considered the leader and I definitely didn't want to appear weak in front of my co-workers. I believed that I needed to keep this a secret so that I would not lose the respect of my employees. In addition, I did not want my superiors to know because I thought I might lose my job if they found out.

After a few months of agonizing over these questions I knew that I had to take the chance and try therapy. I didn't have any other choice. It was seek help or die - there was no gray area. I decided that I definitely wanted to live, and I somehow gained the courage to seek a therapist.

My first attempt at therapy did not go well. I walked into the therapist's office and pretended that I was seeking information for a friend. I'm sure the people there knew this was a lie, but they allowed me to walk out with some of their brochures and a phone number to their suicide hotline.

To be honest, I was absolutely terrified. But although I was scared, deep down I knew that I would have to gain the courage to try again. I waited a few days and tried a different therapist office. This time I had a completely different result.

As I walked into the office I believe the receptionist picked up on my fear. I began asking her questions about depression and whether or not they had any books that I could read. All of a sudden a therapist walked out and began asking me questions. "May I help you?" she asked. "Not really, I'm just looking for a little information about depression." "Are you depressed?" "I'm not really sure," I answered. "Why don't you come inside and let's talk a little. Is that alright?" "I guess so."

As I followed her into her office it felt as if my heart was going to jump out of my chest. I was so nervous and afraid that I was literally dripping with sweat. She obviously picked up on this and began to put my mind at ease.

"What is your name?"

"Michael."

"Well Michael, I can sense that you are a little nervous, so let me start by asking what I can do to help you. Is there anything I can do for you?"

"Well maybe. I have been doing some research about depression and I think I'm depressed, but I'm really not sure."

"Do you feel depressed?"

"Based on what I've read so far I think I am. But to be completely honest I'm not sure I know exactly what depression is supposed to feel like. Does that make any sense to you?"

"It makes a lot of sense to me. Unfortunately most men do not recognize how they feel. Men have been conditioned to disconnect from their emotions and that makes it extremely difficult for them to express how they really feel. Most men will tell you what they think, but they usually do not know how they feel. You apparently fit into this category."

"I'm not sure if I really understand what you're saying, but a part of me thinks that you're right."

"You just validated the point I made. You are currently speaking from an intellectual perspective, instead of an emotional one. It sounds as if you are disconnected from your emotions."

"Let's assume that you're right. If I am disconnected from my emotions, how do I get reconnected? Do you have any books on how to do this?

"Unfortunately you cannot reconnect to your emotions by reading books. In order for you to reconnect you have to relearn how to feel. This can be accomplished through therapy with me or any trained therapist."

"I really don't understand what you mean. But if I decide to relearn how to feel how long will it take?"

"I really can't answer that question. It's really up to you and how committed you are to doing the work."

"What do you mean doing the work? What kind of work is involved?"

"In the therapeutic community we use the word 'work' because it takes a considerable amount of effort to heal yourself so that you can reconnect with your emotions. Doing the work means that you become willing to open yourself up on an emotional level. This can be quite difficult at times."

"Well I believe I'm ready. I'm really tired of being alone and I definitely want to experience some fun in my life again. I think I can do this, so how much will it cost?"

"I operate on a sliding scale based on your ability to pay. The most important thing is for you to make the commitment to yourself to heal and we can address the money issue at a later date. Are you ready to begin? Let's set up a date and time for you to begin your healing."

"I just wanted to thank you for being so nice and understanding. The truth is I was about to run out of your office before you showed up. Now I am really glad that I came because I really believe that you can help me."

"That is a great attitude to have. I'm glad that you trust me enough to work with you. Just remember that I can guide you, but you must be willing to do the work. As long as you believe that you can heal I can assure you that you will. Just stay committed and trust the process and you will be just fine. The truth is you have already done the hard part by showing up today. It takes an incredible amount of courage to be here and I'm proud of you for taking the first step."

As I left the therapist's office that day I knew I had just taken the biggest step of my life. I didn't know what to expect, but I knew I was willing to do whatever it took to heal my emotions and relearn how to feel. I became committed to my own healing, and I can now say that I'm emotionally healed and connected to my authentic self.

As the therapist mentioned, it wasn't easy, but it was definitely possible. It has been one of the most challenging, yet most fulfilling, journeys of my life.

I cannot put into words the joy I feel on a regular basis as a result of carry out my emotional work. My relationships now work, my creativity and sense of reverence is enhanced, my love of nature has been rekindled, and my professional life is rewarding and fulfilling. I took the road less traveled and it has made all the difference in the world for me.

I wanted to share this story because there is such a

negative stigma about men and therapy that I believe it's time for a new conversation. In this new conversation men will recognize the importance of healing their emotions and they will put forth the effort to do their healing work.

When we learn to support each other in our growth we can remove the fear and stigma of being emotionally vulnerable, which will ultimately result in us being happier human beings. I personally believe that this is the most important work men can participate in, and we must begin supporting each other through this process.

If we gain the courage to do this work, we will see a decline in domestic violence, child abuse, alcoholism, and random acts of violence. The time has come for a new conversation about our emotional healing.

Are you willing to join in the conversation?

So the first step in making peace with your past is to make sure that you do some emotional healing work. It may be in the form of therapy, but it could also be through support groups like AA or even workshops such as Landmark Education - landmarkeducation.com.

The key is to become 100% committed to healing your heart and making peace with your past. Once you commit and then take action I can assure you that you will begin to feel better about your life, and it will definitely get easier. It won't be an easy process, but I promise you it will be worth it.

2. Workshops/Seminars/Webinars

The second thing I recommend you do is to be willing to

participate in personal development seminars. If you have never done anything like this before, you're simply going to have to trust me. There are countless seminars available that can support you in making peace with your past. There are one day seminars, three day retreats, online webinars, and a wide variety of others that can assist you along your journey. Here are just a few that I have found extremely helpful.

If you are male, I highly recommend a three-day workshop called The New Warrior Training Adventure. It is carried out by an organization called The Mankind Project, and without question it is one of the most transformational experiences you will ever encounter.

You can find out more about them at:
mankindproject.org.

If you are female, they have a sister organization called The Woman Within, who offer similar training for women, and I'm sure it will be transformational as well.

You can find them at:
womanwithin.org.

There are several organizations that offer inner-child healing workshops around the country. I suggest that you research online for inner child work and find a resource in your area. You will simply have to trust yourself and find one that feels right for you. You can begin by reading some books by John Bradshaw if you aren't comfortable attending the workshops. Two of my favorites are *Healing The Shame That Binds You* and *Homecoming*. I highly recommend that you pick up a copy of both.

The key is to become 100% committed to making peace with your past. You have to want it more than anything. You have to listen to that still small voice within you that is calling you to do this work. It's all up to you!

I am absolutely convinced that making peace with your past is a surefire way to achieve true freedom and happiness. As I've mentioned before, it won't be easy, but it will definitely be worth it. If you commit to doing this I can promise you that you will experience deep inner peace, less anxiety, no more depression, a deeper sense of passion and purpose, and a deep inner knowing that you can create the life of your dreams.

Isn't that what you really want - a more rewarding and fulfilling life experience? If the answer is yes, begin by making peace with your past and I can assure you that you will have everything you need to do so.

I would like to close this chapter with a quote from the Dalai Lama. He was once asked what he found most fascinating about human beings, and this is the answer he gave:

> *"Man sacrifices his health in order to make money. Then he sacrifices money to recuperate his health. And then he is so anxious about the future that he does not enjoy the present moment. As a result, he does not live in the present or the future, he lives as if he is never going to die, and then he dies having never truly lived."*

Make sure you do not make this mistake. If you make peace with your past it will give you lots of reasons to make sure that your life is well lived and that you have absolutely no regrets. Do not die with your music still in you. Learn to sing your song so that the whole world hears you, and you will experience joy that defies human understanding.

Live your life out loud! You can do this!

"Your time is limited, so don't waste it living someone else's life. Don't be trapped by dogma – which is living with the results of other people's thinking. Don't let the noise of other's opinions drown out your own inner voice. And most important, have the courage to follow your heart and intuition."

Steve Jobs

Chapter 4
Intuition/Synchronicity

Have you ever noticed how many "experts" there appears to be throughout media? If you turn on the television right now, chances are you will see an "expert" giving advice or their opinion on a wide range of topics, from politics to religion, to health and fitness, to money to sex, and a multitude of other social issues. But have you ever listened to an "expert" and asked yourself "how in the world did they become an expert when it is pretty obvious that they don't have a clue what they're talking about?" In other words, they may be an "expert," but it was pretty obvious that they had absolutely no common sense.

In a society that creates celebrities out of experts and authors, it's no wonder so many people feel confused and frustrated. We are constantly bombarded with statistics and reports from the so-called "experts" that are supposed to inform us, but ultimately they only confuse us. For example, one expert says that you should not eat meat, and the other says you should. Or one expert says you shouldn't drink alcohol, while another one says that it's actually good for you. For every expert position, there is an opposition, which leads to polarization and ultimately confusion.

So whom are you supposed to trust and believe?

Before I answer that question, let me say, as an author of three books and a radio and TV show host, I have been recognized as an expert on several different occasions. It's actually a title that I've never been completely comfortable with, but because of my knowledge and experience I have accepted the title. So my intention here is not to attack experts in any way, I just want to make you aware that anyone can become an expert, but just because they have that title and some credentials does not mean that they necessarily know what's best for you.

In order for you to be truly happy with yourself and your life, it is your responsibility to become the "expert" of you. The one person that you must learn to trust and believe is yourself. This doesn't mean that you can't listen to, and learn from, the experts - it means that no one should know you better than you know yourself.

Brendon Burchard, the creator of a program called the Expert Academy, created a definition of "expert" that I really align with: "An expert is someone who is proficient in 3-R's. Researching, Reporting, and creating Results." This is the best definition of expert that I've ever come across, because it shares a simple truth. If you are willing to do your research and then report what you learn with others, and it helps them create positive results in their lives, then by definition you are an expert. Based on this definition I consider myself to be an expert because for the past twenty years that is exactly what I've been doing. I love doing research and sharing what I've learned, and by sharing my wisdom I support others in creating positive results in their lives.

Based on the researching, reporting, and results I've been responsible for over the past twenty years, I have come to know that if you truly want to be successful and fulfilled in your life, there is one simple thing that you absolutely, positively, must learn how to do, and that is to learn to listen to, and trust, your intuition.

Let me reiterate Steve Jobs' quote:

> "Your time is limited, so don't waste it living someone else's life. Don't be trapped by dogma – which is living with the results of other people's thinking. Don't let the noise of other's opinions drown out your own inner voice. And most important, have the courage to follow your heart and intuition."

I believe the reason so many people are so unhappy with their lives is because they listen to the so-called "experts" and do not know how to listen to their own intuition. With all of the access we have to technology and information, too many of us rely on it to try to find happiness and fulfillment. Some people follow gurus and experts in the hopes of finding happiness, when the reality is that the gurus and experts aren't the real source of happiness. The real source of happiness is within you, and until you look within yourself you will never find it.

Since listening to your intuition is so important, I wanted to take this opportunity to share some things that I have learned about intuition and hopefully provide you with some insights that will help you to get in touch with your own intuition, and then use it to guide you to your ultimate destiny.

So let's begin by defining what intuition really is. Webster's dictionary describes it as: *a natural ability or power that makes it possible to know something without any proof or evidence: a feeling that guides a person to act a certain way without fully understanding why.*

In American culture, intuition has usually been associated with women. Have you ever heard the term "woman's intuition"? The truth is, intuition has absolutely nothing to do with gender. I believe men are just as intuitive as women, but unfortunately in our culture men have been conditioned to believe that they aren't.

Although it's somewhat difficult to fully define intuition with words, take a moment and ask yourself if you've experienced any of these situations.

- You were thinking about someone when the phone rings and it turns out to be the person you were thinking about.
- You had a funny feeling in your gut that told you not to do something, even though you wanted to, and then you listened to your gut and it turned out to be right?
- Something happened to you at just the right moment in a way that you didn't expect, but it helped you reach one of your goals.
- You were thinking about a friend or someone you care about that you haven't seen in a while, and then you ran into them at or store or some unexpected place.
- You were struggling with a problem, and all of a sudden a solution popped into your head without you even thinking about it.

If you've experienced any of these situations, you've actually used your intuition. Referring to the quote; *"a feeling that guides a person to act a certain way without fully understanding why"* that feeling or knowing that you had without knowing why was your intuition.

Intuition/Synchronicity

If you accept what I said in the previous chapter about The Source, then another way to look at intuition is simply as The Source's way of communicating directly with you. I believe that we all have direct access to The Source, but unfortunately very few people will tap into it. Since you're reading this book, I'm going to assume that you would like to access your intuition, so let me share *5 Ways To Help You Get In Touch With Your Intuition* by Christina Lattimer of People Discovery Magazine.

1. Meditation is giving you a holiday from the clamor of your daily thoughts and stream of information. It is finding the gap between your thoughts and staying there. Silent and observant, you can watch your thoughts without attaching yourself to them. It is allowing your intuition or your unconscious wisdom space. Through mediation, your intuition may come to you in different ways, either through thoughts, ideas, or an encounter with someone or something. Use meditation to be open to whatever comes up.

2. Contemplation is also about clearing your mind, but for me it is more purposeful. You may have a problem or a situation where you're not sure what to do, or don't know what the solution is. Ask clearly what the problem is, and then simply observe the problem from different angles and instead of actively thinking about the information, let thoughts come up. Often, you can be inspired with a solution, although sometimes the emerging solution isn't immediate. It can pop up at any time.

3. Writing is extremely powerful if you are disturbed or upset, even if you aren't sure why. Write down how you are feeling, why you are feeling that way, and then ask your intuition how you can look at the situation differently. Then write down different ideas, until you find a perspective which feels good and you can believe. Writing is about telling the story of what is going on in your mind and giving you an opportunity to <u>see it from a better perspective</u>. The true trick is to ask your intuition how to perceive the situation so that you can be at peace with it. It's not about repressing feelings though. Feelings are a great emotional guidance system, and it's important to let them come up and help to inform the writing process.

4. Listen to Music – You are better aligned with your intuition or higher self when you are feeling good. You know you are feeling good when you are in touch with appreciation, gratitude, love, and laughter. Listening to music you love can quickly help you get into those places which feel so good. A daily dose of music you love can definitely align you with your intuition.

5. Going outside – Whether it's fresh winter air or warm summer sunshine, getting away from the clutter of a busy workplace or a demanding home can clear your mind and give you space which you might not otherwise give yourself. Staying in the present moment and clearing your mind while you are outside is a must. It's no good getting out into the open and taking all your clamorous thoughts with you.

If you take the time to make peace with your past and carry out your emotional healing work that I mentioned earlier, I believe it will definitely support you in getting in touch with your intuition. Carrying out your deep inner work is like cleaning out the pipe I mentioned, which is your connection to The Source. When that pipe is clear, your intuition flows freely back and forth from The Source, which is the key to tapping into your intuition.

I ran across a very informative article titled *10 Things Highly Intuitive People Do Differently*, by Carolyn Gregoire of the Huffington Post Magazine, which shared some amazing insights about intuition. I would like to share her 10 things, and then share my comments about them.

1. They listen to that inner voice.
2. They take time for solitude.
3. They create.
4. They practice mindfulness.
5. They observe everything.
6. They listen to their bodies.
7. They connect deeply with others.
8. They pay attention to their dreams.
9. They enjoy plenty of down time.
10. They mindfully let go of negative emotions.

1. They listen to that inner voice.

This is the key to developing your intuition. The more you listen to it, the more you will be able to recognize it. I now trust my intuition more than I trust my logical mind. If something doesn't feel right, yet makes logical sense, I will pay more attention to the feeling than I will the logical thought. My inner voice is the guiding force in all of my decisions.

2. They take time for solitude.

I am naturally a loner. This does not mean that I'm antisocial, it simply means that I always make time for personal solitude. As a matter of fact, I am an extroverted guy who really loves being around people, but I also value my solitude and love spending time alone. As a happily married man I love spending time with my wife, but she also recognizes my need for solitary time and she allows me to have it on a regular basis without feeling neglected. It's an extremely important part of my life.

3. They create.

I am highly creative and absolutely love creating new things. Whether it's writing books, developing programs, or creating motivational speeches, I have to express my creativity. As I tap into my intuition it gives me access to an infinite amount of creative ideas.

4. They practice mindfulness.

Mindfulness is the practice of being aware. It's about paying attention and being in the present moment. It means being in touch with your thoughts, feelings, and physical sensations, and recognizing that what happens to me doesn't matter, as much as what I do with what happens to me.

5. They observe everything.

I try to maintain a childlike curiousness in everything I do. This keeps me open minded and aware of everything around me. I'm like a sponge in any environment, simply taking in everything that's going around me and being able to make conscious choices in how I react to those things.

6. They listen to their bodies.

Being in touch with my physical body is a high priority for me. I enjoy working out and taking care of my body and I have learned to listen to it when it sends me signals that something may be wrong. I also get a yearly physical, which gives me an idea of what's going on in my body to make sure that I prevent any problems that may arise. I'm a firm believer in the philosophy that an ounce of prevention is worth a pound of cure.

7. They connect deeply with others.

Having deep and intimate connected relationships is the foundation of my happiness. Learning how to do this took years of deep inner emotional and psychological work, but the results have been amazing. Learning to open my heart to others to give and receive love brings me great joy.

8. They pay attention to their dreams.

Having dreams and goals are another driving force in my life. As an entrepreneur, I am constantly seeking new ways to grow my business and build my legacy. All my entrepreneurial pursuits are driven by my commitment to making the world a better place by sharing my unique gifts and talents with the world.

9. They enjoy plenty of down time.

Down time for me is watching movies, listening to '70s soul music, and reading my favorite comic strip, Calvin & Hobbes. It's also spending time in silence through my meditation practice. I make a point to do at least one of these every single day.

10. They mindfully let go of negative emotions.

I am a huge advocate of personal development programs that help heal emotional and psychological trauma. I have spent a considerable amount of time, energy, and effort letting go of negative emotions and as a result it has brought me deep inner peace and serenity, and it has definitely connected me to my intuition.

If you make the commitment to yourself to get in touch with your intuition, you too can enjoy all ten of these things. Anyone can do this; they simply have to make a commitment to access their intuition and make it a high priority in their lives.

There are countless benefits to connecting with your intuition, but by far I believe the greatest benefit is becoming aware of divine synchronicities. When and if you truly tap into your intuition it will serve as a guidance system for your life. When you do this, you will begin to recognize how unexplainable coincidences are actually divine synchronicities set in motion by The Source, and your intuition helps you to recognize them.

Rather than try to define synchronicities, I would like to share a series of synchronicities that confirm for me that The Source was constantly working in my favor to support me in manifesting a lifelong dream of mine.

More than twenty years ago I had a dream to run a company that would develop self-esteem building programs for children. I had no experience in developing programs and I had no idea how to start a non-profit organization that would implement these programs. Despite my lack of knowledge and experience I decided that I would start a company anyway. After several years of failure I held on to my dream of building this company, but the reality was my life had actually fallen apart. I got to a point where I was homeless for a couple of years, and despite the challenges I still held on to the dream.

Approximately seven years after I had conceived the idea for my company, I had no luck in getting it funded. Despite this, I held on to my dream and continued to look for ways to bring my dream to reality. During this time I was renting a rundown one-room apartment and I was making minimum wage working at a video store. I had a bicycle for transportation and I could barely make ends meet. But somehow I intuitively knew that I would eventually figure out a way to raise the money for my company.

One day while working at the video store, a man came in with his children and asked me if I could make a recommendation for some movies for them to watch. I made the recommendation and he took them home to view them with his children.

A couple of days later he came back and told me that his children absolutely loved the movies and he wanted to thank me for the recommendations. He then became a regular customer that would always come in on the weekends and pick up movies to watch.

One evening he came in and we started talking, and somehow we began talking about challenges in life. He then told me that he was dealing with a major challenge because he had recently been diagnosed with cancer. During our conversation I mentioned some of the challenges I had gone through, and I suggested to him that no matter how difficult challenges might be, there is always a positive lesson for us to learn within them.

When I said that, he smiled at me and said he completely agreed. He told me how his diagnosis had challenged him to really take a deep look at his life, and since he had been diagnosed he had actually been happier with his life because for the first time he realized just how important his children were and how precious his life was. As a result of his cancer he had become a better father, and ultimately a better man.

After our conversation we became close friends and each time he would visit we would spend some time just chatting and supporting each other.

One day I was at work with a co-worker and my friend came in and asked for some movie recommendations. After he picked up his movies and left, my co-worker asked me if I knew who he was. I told him yes, and said that he was a friend of mine. My co-worker then asked me again, "Do you realize who that is?" I said yes, his name is Mike and he is a good customer and a good friend of mine.

My co-worker then informed me that he was a very wealthy businessman who owned an oil company.

The next time my friend came in the store I decided to ask him if he might be able to help me with my dream. I told him about my dream of creating the programs for kids and I asked him if there was any way that he could help out.

He then reached into his pocket and handed me one of

his business cards. "Michael, whatever you're working on I would be glad to help you. Contact my secretary and make an appointment and let me see what I can do."

During this time I was deeply involved with spiritual teachings and I had learned to keep my heart and my mind open to miracles. I didn't know how he would help me, but I intuitively knew that somehow he would.

A few days later I met him at his office and I was pleasantly surprised to learn just how wealthy he was. His office was like something you would see on a television set. It was filled with sports memorabilia, wild animals, and pictures of my friend with former presidents and lots of famous celebrities.

I sat down and began explaining my idea to him. After I finished, he picked up the phone and contacted another wealthy businessman who was in charge of a non-profit foundation that had access to lots of money. He told the person on the phone that I would be coming by to visit him and that he wanted to make sure that he would support my programs.

When he hung up the phone he gave me another business card and told me to make an appointment to see the guy he had just spoken with, and he assured me that the man would be able to help me in some way. I thanked him repeatedly and let him know just how much I appreciated his support. He then looked at me and said *"I want to thank you for being my friend and for listening to me and sharing your dreams with me. I believe you are going to be very successful and I'm glad that I was able to help."*

A few weeks later I met with the other businessman who loved my business idea, and a few months later I received a check for fifty thousand dollars to get my company started.

Let that sink in for a moment. I was completely broke, I had no formal education or training, I had a bicycle for transportation, and I was living in a rundown dilapidated apartment that I could barely afford. Despite all of these challenges I was able to receive a check for fifty thousand dollars!

A lot of people would say that this was just coincidence or I was just lucky. I, on the other hand, recognize that this had absolutely nothing to do with luck. It was divine synchronicity that orchestrated all of the events that led to me receiving the funding. It began with my belief that I would receive the funding. Faith is defined as evidence of things unseen, and I had unwavering faith that somehow I would be able to secure funding. It was then followed by my willingness to work extremely hard to keep my head above water while I was trying to start my company.

My faith and belief in The Source and myself gave me the patience and persistence to not give up even after several years of failure. The key was my willingness to listen to my intuition and to trust that The Source would provide me with the guidance I needed to be at the right place at the right time to meet the right people. By relying on The Source 100% and being willing to combine action with faith, I was able to locate the funding to get my company started.

This is why it is so important to learn to listen to, and

trust, your intuition. As I've mentioned, The Source is constantly communicating with us through our intuition, and when we tune in and learn to connect the dots of synchronicity, The Source can guide us to our ultimate destiny.

So learn to listen to your heart and connect to your intuition, and you will receive all the guidance you need to live the life of your dreams.

I'm living proof of this.

"Your work is not to drag the world kicking and screaming into a new awareness. Your job is to simply do your work. Sacredly, Secretly and Silently. And those with eyes to see and ears to hear will respond."

The Arcturians

Chapter 5
Cultural Conditioning/Programming

I recently read a Gallup poll that stated 70% of Americans either hated their job, or were disengaged from their work. Wow, 70% - that's unbelievable to me!

Why is that? Why are so many people working at jobs they hate? How is it that we are one of the richest countries on the planet and yet the overwhelming majority of us are doing work that we hate? If we really hate our jobs, how effective can we be at them? How wealthy would this country be if 70% of the workforce loved their jobs and actually enjoyed going to work every day? Don't you think that would have a positive impact on our economy? I certainly do!

Rather than focus on the problem, I'd like to focus on solutions, so let's ask a different question: is it possible to create a job that you love? Is it possible for a person to have a vocation that lights them up and gets them up in the morning with excitement and passion?

I believe the answer is yes. Not only is it possible, it is actually mandatory if you truly want to live an extraordinary life. A key component of being happy is to be able to say that you truly enjoy your work; it shouldn't matter so much about what you do, what's more important is how you do it. For example, you could be working at McDonalds flipping burgers and you could actually be happy with your job. You do not have to make millions of dollars to be happy, you simply have to have the right attitude and mindset about whatever it is you're doing. It's all in your attitude, which will always determine your altitude.

Like most people, I've worked at jobs that I truly disliked, but even if I didn't necessarily like the job, I made it a point to always have a positive attitude about it. Whenever it got to a point where my attitude towards the job turned negative, I knew that it was time to find another job.

As a writer, radio host, and motivational speaker who has literally read hundreds of books and attended hundreds of hours of seminars, as well as interviewing some of the brightest minds in human behavior and personal development, I have come to the conclusion that the primary reason so many people are unhappy with their work and their lives is because of unconscious human conditioning or programming.

Before I explain what conditioning/programming is, I would like to share a metaphorical story that actually summarizes how human conditioning works. This is a story that I wrote that really reflects how I felt when I was experiencing a lot of adversity in my own life. I'd like for you to take a moment after you read it and see if you can relate.

~ ~ ~

The Rollercoaster

I had heard a lot about the rollercoaster. Initially I didn't want to go and see it, but everyone kept saying, "You have to check it out and get on it. It will be so much fun."

Reluctantly, I went to see it. It was intriguing and enticing and it looked like fun.

"You have to get on it!" everyone said.

Cultural Conditioning/Programming

"I'm not sure that I want to."

"But everyone loves getting on the Rollercoaster," they said.

"I don't think I'll like it."

"Go ahead and try it, you'll like it," everyone said.

So I tried it.

At the beginning it was fun. Going round and round and up and down with friends who also seemed to be having fun was initially enjoyable.

But after a short while, I got bored and tired. I didn't want to ride it any more. I decided that I wanted to get off.

"You can't get off," everyone said.

"But I'm ready to."

"No one gets off the rollercoaster once they get on."

"Why not?"

"They just don't."

"But I'm ready to get off."

"Why not ride it a little longer and see if you'll change your mind?" they said.

"Okay, I'll try it a little longer."

Round and round, up and down I went pretending that I was enjoying myself.

But after a while I began to get angry. I was tired of the rollercoaster and I realized that I shouldn't have got on it in the first place. I wanted to get off, but I didn't know how.

"I'm really sick of this rollercoaster. I want to get off right now."

"We're sorry but you must stay on the rollercoaster. That's the rule."

"Well I guess I'm going to have to break the rule because I'm about to get off."

"But if you break the rule no one will like you and you will probably get hurt," they said.

"I don't care about anyone else. I want to get off now. Who can I talk to about getting off this thing?"

"No one knows how to get off," they said.

"I'm sure someone knows, I just have to find them."

"It's been said that only a few people have ever got off this rollercoaster. And no one really knows what happened to them. Some believe that people have even been killed trying to get off. Why take that risk?"

"At this point I'm willing to take that risk. I don't care what people think or what people are going to say. I refuse to keep going round and round and getting nowhere on this thing, and I must do something to get off."

I didn't know what to do, but I knew that I couldn't stay on the rollercoaster. I needed a plan and I needed it

Cultural Conditioning/Programming

soon. I felt as though I was dying and I really wanted to live again.

But what about the risk? What if what they say is true? What if I really can't get off or what if I get killed trying to get off?

At this point I decide that I have only one choice. And that choice is to live. I don't know what is going to happen, but I know if I stay on this thing I'm already dead. I have to trust my inner instincts and take the chance and simply jump off. I'm not sure where I'll land or if I'll get hurt or even die, but I just know that I have to jump.

So despite what everyone else were saying and the fear and uncertainty I felt, I took a deep breath and jumped. As my body was hurled through the air uncontrollably, surprisingly I felt a deep sense of calm and inner peace, and then I did exactly what I intuitively knew I could do - I flew!

~ ~ ~

So, can you relate to the story? Have you ever felt as if you were trapped on the rollercoaster and couldn't get off? Let's break down the story and get a better understanding of how human conditioning and programming works.

At the beginning of the story I was paying more attention to what other people were saying instead of trusting my own instincts about the rollercoaster. Like too many people, we get tangled up in peer pressure and pay more attention to what others think and say than listening to our own inner voices. When I decided to get off, I was initially more concerned with what other people would say and think, and that's the reason that I stayed on the rollercoaster longer than I really wanted to.

It wasn't until I got bored and angry that I began to gain the courage to go against what everyone else was doing and saying. Once the boredom and pain became too great, I made a simple choice. I was able to let go of my need to meet other people's approval and trust my gut to do what was right for me. At that point I was willing to accept the consequences of my choices and I trusted my own heart to make the choice to jump. Jumping into the great unknown is what keeps most people trapped in lives of mediocrity and discontent.

The driving factor is fear. We are afraid of the unknown and uncertainty, and for some people it feels safer to just stay on the rollercoaster and do what everyone else is doing. By trusting my own inner wisdom and letting go of the need to meet other people's approval, I was able to embrace my fears and move through them. Once I did this, I experienced true internal freedom, which allowed me to fly away and to become the man I knew that I could be.

In summary, this is the key to living the life you were born to live. You must be willing to trust your own inner wisdom and not allow others to dictate what you can or cannot do. You must be willing to face all your fears and most importantly, you must be willing to accept the consequences of your choices. As soon as you do this, you will be free and ready to fly.

Let's take a look at how and why human conditioning

and programming is so important to understand.

As human beings, we receive most of our programming through three primary sources; our families, our culture, and our society.

Our Families

Without question our families have the biggest impact on our conditioning. As mentioned in the chapter *Who Are You*, when we are first born our subconscious minds are like video recorders that are simply recording all events and experiences in our lives, and then our conscious mind begins creating beliefs about those prerecorded tapes.

Another way to look at it is as if our brains are like computers. When you first build a computer it has no information stored on it - it's basically just an empty mechanical box. Your brain is basically the same. It is a completely blank slate when you're born, so your brain is the hardware, your subconscious mind is the operating system, and your conscious mind are the programs that you run.

Your subconscious mind (operating system) is the most powerful part of you because it stores how you feel and what you believe about yourself. Although it runs in the background it has the biggest impact on your behavior because it is 1000% more powerful than your conscious mind.

All the programming that you receive about yourself between the ages of birth and seven will be the filters through which you see the world. In other words, if your programming from your family is that you are a smart, lovable, and caring, all your life experiences will generally be processed through that belief. On the other hand, if the programming is that you are stupid, violent, and unlovable, guess how you're going to show up in the world?

Our Culture

If you are born into a Native American culture your programming will be different from someone born into a Japanese culture. When you consider things like religion, morality, sexuality, and community, each culture has a slightly different set of programming within it. We are all heavily influenced by the cultures we are born into, and our cultural program is embedded into our subconscious mind, and they become our cultural beliefs, which dictate a lot of our behaviors.

Our Society

If you turn on the television you will be exposed to a wide variety of societal conditioning that has a major impact on our lives. If you think deeply about this, a society is simply a reflection of the consciousness of its people, and without question the consciousness of America is driven by violence. Most people may not admit this, or are not aware of this, but America is a culture that absolutely loves violence. How do I know this? Simply take a look at our media. Results don't lie. Although most people in this country talk about wanting peace, the truth is, our society as a collective loves violence. Take a look at our movies or listen to our music, what sells the most? Movies and music filled with violence.

Think about how our government approaches social

issues. Collectively speaking we're always trying to fight things. For example, we have a war on poverty, a war on drugs, a war on illiteracy, a military budget that is 54% of our total federal budget, and the U.S. has the highest firearm-related homicide rate among developed nations. We live in a society that collectively loves violence, so it should come as no surprise that its inhabitants are so violent. The conditioning and programming in America is violent.

Whether you believe it or not, this violence has an impact on the majority of people. Either they will act out in violent ways, become apathetic or indifferent about the violence, or simply deny that it exists. But the fact remains America is a very violent country.

We also happen to be one of the most materialistic countries on the planet. If you watch our commercials you should recognize how marketing experts influence our behavior by constantly bombarding us with images of materialism and consumerism. We are taught that if we truly love someone, we buy him or her a diamond. If we love our kids then we buy them iPhones or PlayStations. We are constantly pursuing "more" and "bigger" everything. We want more stuff and bigger houses, and we believe that these things will make us happy. The sad part is when we accomplish these things and realize that they don't make us happy, we end up becoming angry or upset, which feeds right back into the materialism and consumerism that causes us so much unhappiness in the first place.

Rest assured that I am not bashing America here. I love this country and I believe capitalism is a very good thing. I do not believe that America is on the decline; I simply believe that we are waking up to a new level of consciousness that will support us in creating a more positive, less violent and less materialistic society filled with empathy and compassion. When we do this, we will begin to see the eradication of the majority of the social ills that currently plague our country.

The point I'm making is that our conditioning and programming has a direct impact on our lives, and if you aren't aware of it, it will cause you a lot of pain and discomfort. The key is for you to wake up and break free from the conditioning/programming and ensure that you're completely aware and conscious of the choices you make in life. If you aren't, then it's quite possible that you will blame society and other people for your failure, and that's not what you should want to do.

Remember what I said in chapter one about the first thing you have to do to turn adversity into allies? **You must take 100% responsibility for your life.** Are you ready to do that? If the answer is yes, let's look at the 5 things you must do to break free from societal conditioning and programming.

1. You must be willing to wake up and become aware of your current conditioning.

The key to making any changes in your life is awareness. You can't change something about yourself that you aren't aware of. Awareness means becoming conscious of the subconscious. Remember what I said about the brain working like a computer? That's the good news, because if you aren't happy with the programs on a computer you can simply delete them and purchase new ones.

Cultural Conditioning/Programming

Your brain works the same way. You can rewrite the scripts and change any of the prerecorded tapes that may be in your subconscious. It doesn't matter what you may have learned or believe about yourself, if you truly want to change your internal programs you can do so. In the chapter about Making Peace With Your Past, I shared several ways that you can change your internal and subconscious programs. I highly recommend that you reread that chapter if you're committed to changing your programming.

I have to admit that this may not be easy. As a matter of fact, it could possibly be the most difficult thing that you've ever done - but you can rest assured that if you do this you can expect to experience unprecedented levels of joy, serenity, and inner peace.

But you must be willing to do the work.

The most difficult part will be to get the ego part of yourself to work with you, not against you. Your ego is the part of you that will try to convince you that you do not need to change. It will be that little voice in your head that says you can't do this. It will come up with all sorts of excuses to keep you from changing, so you must learn to recognize it and not listen to it. It will analyze and rationalize everything and convince you to stay the same, so you must be diligent in your commitment to change, which leads us to step two in changing your programming.

2. You must put together a positive system to support you in changing your programming.

It is imperative that you surround yourself with like-minded people if you are committed to changing your programming. With all the negative programming you receive from your family, your culture, and society, you must have associates, friends, and family members who believe that change is possible and will support you in changing. This can be difficult because unfortunately most people aren't willing to change. You will also need support to help you to keep your ego in check. When that little voice inside your head starts telling you what you can't do, a support system can help you change that voice to say that you can.

I'm reminded of a quote from the movie *The Matrix* in which one of the characters says:

> *"That system is our enemy. But when you're inside, you look around, what do you see? Businessmen, teachers, lawyers, carpenters. The very minds of the people we are trying to save. But until we do, these people are still a part of that system and that makes them our enemy. You have to understand, most of these people are not ready to be unplugged. And many of them are so inert, so hopelessly dependent on the system that they will fight to protect it."*

The truth is, most people will fight for their subconscious programming, and they are completely unaware that they are doing so. People will do everything in their power to try to keep you trapped in their limited belief systems, so it's important that you find people who are on the same path as you - people who are willing to look at the world a little differently and aren't afraid to go against the status quo.

Oprah Winfrey once said "Surround yourself only with

people who are willing to take you higher." This is a powerful statement and one that you should abide by.

Building a support system also includes participating in workshops and seminars that support you in changing your programming. There are an unlimited amount of resources available to you, so you must simply commit to finding one that works. You can check out a list of resources at the end of this book if you're not sure where to begin.

3. You must be willing to become open-minded and change some of your programming.

It's been said that the mind is like a parachute; it only works when it's open. This applies to changing your programming. Having an open mind means you are willing to examine some of your deeply held beliefs about yourself and the world around you. In some cases this may cause a strain on your relationships with friends and family, but you must stay the course. You must make a choice that you are at least willing to look at your current programming, and then make changes if needed. The difficult part is that you must be willing to examine things that you don't know *you don't know*.

As an example, when I started this process more than twenty years ago, I had absolutely no idea that my childhood beliefs were affecting me as an adult. I didn't know just how much I *didn't know* about myself, but I was willing to learn. I was willing to do whatever it took to figure out how to become happy with my life, and I simply made it my highest priority. I had no idea what to expect, but I intuitively knew that I wanted and needed to change, so that's what I did. I made the commitment to myself that I was going to change and it allowed me to do just that. You must commit to becoming open-minded and willing to change your programming.

4. You must be willing to journal and reflect on your subconscious beliefs in order to change them.

One of the most powerful ways for you to uncover hidden subconscious beliefs is through journaling. From my own experience I can say that journaling is a powerful tool that can help you to change your programming. I would like to share an article from the website **journalingsaves.com** which is really helpful in getting started with journaling. If you would like more information, check out their website.

~ ~ ~

How to Journal in 10 Simple Steps

If you don't have time to read this whole guide, stick with #1 and you'll do just fine!

1. Keep it simple

Journal writing at its core is simple. You get some paper and a pen, you write a few pages about what's going on, and you do it again tomorrow, and the next day.

We humans are a curious bunch — we make things needlessly complicated. So if you feel yourself getting mired in whether or not you're doing it right, what kind of journal to use, when you "should" write, or if the color of your pen will affect the outcome, take a breath and get back to basics.

Words on a page. It's really that simple.

2. Keep it private

Don't share your journal and shelve it out of reach. Your journaling privacy is essential to the process. Your journal is a safe place for you to explore whatever is on your mind without worrying about how it will affect anyone else. If you fear it will be read, you'll censor yourself and the benefits of journaling will be lost.

Sharing your journal also opens it up for debate and criticism, neither of which are appropriate for this medium. It's nobody's business but yours.

When you're not writing, keep your journal out of sight - it'll at least keep the honest people out.

3. Do it frequently

Writing frequently supports the habit part of journaling. It allows you to witness the ebb and flow of your life and it gives you the perspective that you won't always feel this way — after all, you didn't feel this way yesterday.

Daily journaling provides the most benefits and the best results. If you only write when you "need to," you will forever be in crisis management. Your journal will be filled with dire consequences and high stakes, and you'll continue to live in reactionary mode.

The beauty of frequent journaling is that it helps you to grow as a person, it helps you recognize patterns in your life, and it helps you to gain perspective and control over your environment.

On the other hand, just do your best. If you can't make time for journaling *every* day, do it as often as you can. A couple of times a week is better than not at all, and if you find no time for journaling, just get back to it without beating yourself up.

Journaling should support you and make you feel good. It's not another task to be checked off your list or fodder for self-flagellation when you "fail."

Feeling strapped for time? I hear ya! Even a short journaling session is beneficial if you do it regularly. Free up some time and then try one of these 20 ways to find 20 minutes for journaling. If 20 minutes is beyond you, check out The Lazy Guide to Journaling in 10 Minutes or Less, or just stick to one line a day.

4. Banish the grammar police

Surprisingly, one of the top reasons people cite for not journaling is that they can't spell or their grammar ain't perfect. Since you're journaling for *you* (see #2 above), it doesn't really matter if you dangle your participles or misspell "conjunctivitis." Journaling is not grade school, and nobody's going to hit your knuckles with a ruler.

If you're especially concerned about this, don't re-read your entries for a while - you'll have less opportunity to judge what you've written.

5. Write what you know

Facing the blank page can be overwhelming at first.

When starting your journal, just date the entry and note your location. Start by describing your surroundings if you need to get warmed up. Write a little bit about your day. What's on your mind? Think of your journal like an old friend you're sitting down to coffee with. Just answer, "What's up? What's new? What's going on?"

And if you're afraid you're doing it wrong, I assure you: You are already fabulous!

6. Find the best time and place

You may instinctively know the best time to journal (hint: it's when you'll actually do it!). Look for a natural lull in your day that you can finagle into journaling time. Experiment with morning journaling vs. writing just before bed and see which works best for you.

Find a comfy place to journal where you won't be interrupted. When journal writing at home, it's essential that the few minutes you designate is honored by family, friends, housemates, and pets. Lock the dog in a separate room or get out of the house if you need to and write at a café or the library.

This is *your* time, and you may need to defend it protectively!

7. Write for quantity, not quality

Don't get caught up in how "good" your journal writing is. Nobody cares. Just get it done.

Set goals based on effort — say, three pages or twenty minutes of journaling. Then even if you're convinced your journaling is terrible, you're still successful because you got it done.

Writing quickly for a set period of time is also a way to keep your inner critic at bay, and to banish any negative voices telling you that what you're doing is stupid or that you can't write. Just get the words down and don't worry about how good they are.

The power and beauty of journaling lies in the process, not the product.

8. Try writing by hand

Journaling by hand in a notebook moves a different part of your brain than typing, and before you argue that you can write faster on the computer, journaling is not about speed, efficiency, or volume - it's about dedicating a few minutes each day to honor yourself, your thoughts, and your feelings. Writing by hand helps you to get in touch with all of that better than a keyboard can.

So slow down and savor the process. It builds your brain synapses to hold thoughts in your head long enough to write them down. Journaling by hand will make you smarter (did I mention it will also make you better looking?).

In my journal tour video I illustrate the pros and cons of notebooks I've used through the years. Now I'm faithful to Blueline Notebooks, but it took me twenty years to find my life partner.

Still convinced that you need to journal on the computer? Listen to Podcast #2: Paper vs. Electronic Journals before you decide against journal writing by hand.

9. Keep the stakes low

Don't make any grand announcements before you start journaling. Set yourself up for success by keeping the stakes low. You don't need to proclaim to everyone in your life that you're now a Writer. Don't promise yourself you'll write for one hour every day for rest of your life. Don't expect yourself to churn out the deepest and most poignant journal ever.

Just get a $1 composition book at the drug store and write three pages for as many days this week as you have time for. End of story.

The higher we make the stakes, the more intimidating the process becomes, and the less likely we are to do it, or feel satisfied with the results.

Are there words on that page? If yes, then bam! — instant success.

Wasn't that easy?

10. Enjoy yourself!

Remember that journaling should be enjoyable (most of the time). If you take the task too seriously or put too much pressure on yourself, journaling will become a burden instead of a gift. Keep a spirit of play, and infuse your journal with a little humor. Adding art, creativity, color or heart to your journal keeps the process fresh and inviting.

You'll likely feel awkward and self-conscious when you first start journaling. That's totally fine — you're allowed. Most people are a little awkward and self-conscious when they begin something new, unless they're a freak of nature. It's okay to poke fun at yourself, or to keep the prose light-hearted.

Follow these tips and you'll be on your way to life as a dedicated journaler in no time!

Happy journaling!

~ ~ ~

5. It's a good idea to use affirmations to help you change your programming.

When I first became involved with personal development work I had a friend of mine who suggested that I start using affirmations to help me reprogram my subconscious mind. At first it felt a little weird, but the more I did it, the more comfortable it became. Before long, I was using all sorts of affirmations that really supported me in changing my mindset. In case you're wondering, an affirmation is simply a statement that you repeat over and over again to help you shift your subconscious mind. To give you more insight on why and how they work, I'd like to share a really good article with you about affirmations by Eve Hogan, who is an author and relationship specialist. You can find out more about her at **sacredmauiretreats.com.**

Affirmations: Why They Work & How to Use Them

By Eve Hogan

To "affirm" something, by dictionary definition, means that you are declaring it to be true. So when I affirm that I am fit when I am not, wealthy when I am financially struggling, or loved when I am lonely, how exactly does that work in the guise of living authentically—and who the heck am I kidding?

An affirmation is usually a sentence or phrase that you repeat regularly to make a formal declaration to yourself and the universe of your intention for it to be the truth. While some may say it is akin to "fake it until you make it," I see it a bit more like holding the vision of what I know can be true.

Here is my experience of how they work. We all have in our brains a thing called a Reticular Activating System (RAS), which is like a filter that lets in information that we need, and filters out information that we don't. If we didn't have this system, we would be bombarded with so much information that our senses would overload and we would go into massive overwhelm. Instead, our brain registers what matters to us based on our goals, needs, interests, and desires.

For example, if you and your friend were driving down the street and you were hungry and your friend was looking for a date, you would see all the restaurants (and none of the hot guys or gals) while your friend would see all the potential sweethearts (and none of the restaurants). Most of us have had this experience when a friend shows us their new car and it's a make and model we have never seen before. Then, now that it is important to us, we suddenly begin to see that particular make and model everywhere we look. I used to date a guy who drove a cement truck and would have sworn to you prior to dating him that there were no cement trucks on the public roads and highways where I lived. Once I started dating him, I saw cement trucks everywhere. My reticular activating system recognized what was important to me and allowed the information in.

When you say an affirmation over and over again, a couple of things happen. One is that it sends a very clear message to your RAS that this is important to you. When you do that, it gets busy noticing ways to help you achieve your goals. If ideal weight is your emphasis, you will suddenly begin to see every gym and weight loss product. If money is your goal, investment and earning opportunities will move to the forefront of your awareness. In essence, the affirmation can kick your creativity into high gear.

The other way affirmations work is that they create a dynamic tension in our beings. If what I am saying is at a higher vibration than what I perceive the truth to be, the dynamic tension is uncomfortable. For instance, if I am saying "I am joyfully and healthfully at my ideal weight" when in actuality I am 10, 20, 30+ pounds above my ideal weight, a painful incongruence is felt between what I perceive the truth to be and what I am saying.

Since this is uncomfortable, we want to rid ourselves of the tension. There are only two ways to do that:

one is to stop saying the affirmation; the other is to raise the bar on reality by making the affirmation and reality match.

So what makes an effective affirmation? First, determine what kind of transformation you want to bring about in yourself—a goal or intention. Or determine what quality, attitude, value, or characteristic you want to remind yourself of or develop in yourself. Second, if it fits, add an emotion to the mix or a word that qualities the statement. For instance, I am joyfully at my ideal weight of 125. Or, I'm happily living in my own home. I personally like affirmations that strum my heartstrings: I offer gratitude for every step and every breath. Third, make it positive vs. negative: "I am healthy and fit" rather than "I am no longer fat."

Some say it takes 21 days of repetition for an affirmation make its mark on your psyche, so aim to keep your affirmation going for at least a month. In the beginning you will have to consciously choose to repeat your affirmations. If you repeat them at every opportunity they will begin to replace the negative mind banter that takes over when we are not monitoring our thoughts.

See if you can make the dynamic tension go away by making your words and reality match.

Here are a few positive affirmations to get you started.

- *I am peaceful in my body, heart, and soul.*
- *I easily see the lesson or the blessing in all that is.*

- *Every day, I offer gratitude, trust, and faith for everything that happens in my life.*
- *I am authentic and present.*
- *I am successful in everything I attempt.*
- *I am a magnet for money and abundance.*
- *Love, wisdom, and discernment coexist in my heart.*
- *Deep love is my birthright.*
- *When faced with two choices, I always take the higher path.*
- *I am guided by a higher power.*
- *I am energetic and strong.*
- *I see the best in everyone and they in me.*

Once you get accustomed to doing affirmations, rest assured that they will help you shift your programming in numerous different ways. My favorite affirmation I used when I first got started was; every day in every way I keep getting better and better. By constantly repeating this affirmation in addition to doing some deep emotional healing I was able to transform my programming and my life to become happier and emotionally healthier than I've ever been.

Try it - you'll like it.

So here are the five things you must do to change your programming. Commit to doing them, and your life will change for the better.

1. You must be willing to wake up and become aware of your current conditioning.
2. You must put together a positive system to support you in changing your programming.
3. You must be willing to become open-minded and change some of your programming.
4. You must be willing to journal and reflect on your subconscious beliefs in order to change them.
5. It's a good idea to use affirmations to help you change your programming.

Good luck!

"The great mission of our day is not conquering the sea or space, disease or tyranny. The grand quest which calls to the hero in every one of us is to become fully alive--to stand up and claim our birthright, which is inner freedom, love, and radiant purpose. By fulfilling this, we transform the world."

Jacob Nordby

Chapter 6
The Hero's Journey

Back in 1977 (I was 17 at the time) a friend and I were hanging out late one night and decided we would go check out a movie. Neither of us knew what movie we wanted to see, so we began looking at the movie posters in the theater. I then noticed a poster for a new sci-fi movie that had recently been released and based on the poster it looked pretty interesting. We decided to go and check it out, even though we knew nothing about the movie.

From the very beginning of the movie I knew it was going to be special. I was instantly transported into outer space and the story, actors, visuals, and soundtrack were all out of this world. By the time the movie was over, I had been on an amazing journey that I didn't want to end. I loved the movie so much that I convinced my friend to go back the following night to see it again.

During that summer I ended up watching the movie more than twenty times in the theater. I couldn't stop watching it. Each time I watched it I discovered something new, and after each viewing I couldn't wait to see it again.

It may sound a little odd, but the movie somehow changed my life. It gave me a new perception of reality, and as a result of watching it so many times my attitude changed about the Universe and my place within it.

The movie was Star Wars and even today it is my all-time favorite movie. I still watch it once or twice a year.

The most intriguing concept of the movie was "The Force", which was defined as a universal energy that is within all things and controls all things. The primary character of the movie was Luke Skywalker, and the movie follows him as he learns how to access The Force within him and how he ultimately uses it to save humanity from an evil character named Darth Vader, who used The Force for evil unlike Luke, who used the force for good.

What really caught my attention after the movie came out was the amount of religious leaders who were using the movie to promote their religion and were actually referring to "The Force" as a metaphor for their God. During this time I was more of an agnostic and I really didn't believe in God; it was the non-religious message in the movie that actually attracted me. I really resonated with the idea that every human being has access to this Force and you didn't have to be religious to connect with it. You simply had to learn how to access it and believe in it and it would become a source of amazing abilities and powers.

I had been doing some research about science and physics and there were some very interesting ideas that I had been exposed to that seemed to confirm what The Force in the movie was actually talking about. It reminded me of a famous quote from Albert Einstein (my favorite scientist) in which he stated, "Everything is energy that's just the way that it is. Match the frequency of the reality that you want to create and there is no way that you can't create that reality. It can be no other way. This isn't philosophy, this is physics."

My interpretation of this quote is that The Force is the

divine energy of the Universe. It is the animating force of life and it is actually the Source of all things. I believe every human being has direct access to this energy and it is our responsibility to learn how to access it and use it for our highest good.

Approximately twenty years after falling in love with Star Wars I discovered what it was that compelled me to have such a deep connection and infatuation with the movie.

I was flipping through the channels on television and I ran across an interview between Bill Moyers and a man named Joseph Campbell. Mr. Campbell was a mythologist who had been studying religion, philosophy, and science, and he created a theory that he called the mono-myth. His theory suggested that the overwhelming majority of movies/myths contained a common theme or story. He coined the term *The Hero's Journey* to explain his theory.

As I listened to the interview I had the same feeling of fascination and wonderment that I had when I watched Star Wars for the very first time. I was absolutely entranced with his ideas and belief systems, which were definitely congruent with my own. It turns out that Star Wars was actually based on Mr. Campbell's theory of the Hero's Journey. His work had had a huge impact on the creator of Star Wars, George Lucas. As Mr. Campbell explained his theory and philosophy, my love and fascination with Star Wars deepened, and the reason why I loved it became abundantly clear.

Although I didn't recognize it at the time, I had already began my own Hero's Journey. I had intuitively recognized the deeper meaning in the movie and there was a part of me that knew that I would one day become aware of this journey and ultimately use the theory as the foundation for creating the life of my dreams.

After listening to the interview, I begin reading more about Mr. Campbell and his theory, and I have to credit him with being a mentor and resource of motivation and inspiration as I learned how to use his 12 stages of the Hero's Journey to help me rebuild my life.

Learning how to apply his theory to my own life really supported me in turning my adversities into allies, and I am deeply grateful that I was introduced to his work. My life has been so powerfully impacted by his theory that I have chosen to include it in this book because I know that once embraced, becoming aware of your own Hero's Journey can become a powerful and positive source of wisdom that will guide you to live the life you were born to live.

To do this, you must understand and accept a very simple premise. You are a Hero, and whether you believe it or not, you are on a journey. The questions you must ask yourself right now is are you willing to become conscious of the journey you're on, or are you going to stay unconscious? The fact that you are reading these words right now at this particular time tells me that you are ready to become conscious, and are ready to embark on your own Hero's Journey, so now I would like to share the 12 stages of the Hero's Journey to support you along the way.

To support you in fully understanding the journey, I am going to share some insights I've gained over the past twenty years of my own journey. As you read the 12 stages and then my commentary, take a moment to reflect on both. See if you recognize any similarities in your own life and try to identify where you are on your journey.

1. Ordinary World

This is where the Hero exists before his present story begins, oblivious of the adventures to come. It's his safe place. His everyday life where we learn crucial details about our Hero, his true nature, capabilities, and outlook on life. This anchors the Hero as a human, just like you and me, and makes it easier for us to identify with him and hence later, empathize with his plight.

At this stage in my own life I was trapped on the societal rollercoaster. I was 23-years-old and I had done everything society said I was supposed to do to be successful. All of my energy was focused on making money and accumulating material things. I had worked extremely hard to climb the corporate ladder and I had been rewarded with a great salary, purchasing my first home, and having a wife and kids. Although on the outside it looked like I had the ideal life, on the inside, in my heart and mind, I knew something was missing. But I didn't have a clue what that something was.

2. Call to Adventure

The Hero's adventure begins when he receives a call to action, such as a direct threat to his safety, his family, his way of life, or to the peace of the community in which he lives. It may not be as dramatic as a gunshot, but simply a phone call or conversation, but whatever the call is, and however it manifests itself, it ultimately disrupts the comfort of the Hero's Ordinary World and presents a challenge or quest that must be undertaken.*

My call to adventure began at the age of 29. My American Dream had turned into a nightmare as I experienced the pain, humiliation, and frustration of a divorce, bankruptcy, foreclosure, and a deep state of depression. It was the most dark, difficult, and challenging time of my life. There were times when the pain was so great that I even contemplated taking my own life. Despite the pain and suffering I experienced, I now realize that this is the time in my life when I received my call to adventure. There was a part of me that intuitively knew that I wasn't living up to my full potential and I finally realized just how unhappy I was with my life. I refer to my divorce as my wakeup call, and now in retrospect I can clearly see that my divorce and all of the pain I experienced were actually the best things that could have happened to me.

3. Refusal of the Call

Although the Hero may be eager to accept the quest, at this stage he will have fears that need overcoming. Second thoughts or even deep personal doubts as to whether or not he is up to the challenge. When this happens, the Hero will refuse the call, and as a result may suffer somehow. The problem he faces may seem too much to handle and the comfort of home far more attractive than the perilous road ahead. This would also be our own response and once again helps us bond further with the reluctant Hero.

After my divorce my primary focus was to simply put my life back together. I had to confront the fact that I was unhappy in my career and I was truly ready to do something different with my life. Although it appeared to be irrational at the time, I decided to quit my job and start my own company. Unfortunately, things did not go the way I planned, and after approximately six months I was in even worse shape. My life was spiraling out of control and I couldn't see a way out.

4. Meeting the Mentor

At this crucial turning point where the Hero desperately needs guidance he meets a mentor figure who gives him something he needs. He could be given an object of great importance, insight into the dilemma he faces, wise advice, practical training, or even self-confidence. Whatever the mentor provides the Hero with it serves to dispel his doubts and fears and give him the strength and courage to begin his quest.

I reached a point in my life where I had two choices; get help or die. There was no gray area. I was in such deep emotional, psychological, and physical pain that I knew that I could no longer deal with it all on my own. I gained the courage to go to therapy and began my internal journey of transformation. My therapist was able to help me identify the cause of a lot of my dysfunctional behavior, and she gave me some insights that helped me alleviate my depression and I eventually began to feel happy and hopeful again.

5. Crossing the Threshold

The Hero is now ready to act upon his call to adventure and truly begin his quest, whether it be physical, spiritual, or emotional. He may go willingly or he may be pushed, but either way he finally crosses the threshold between the world he is familiar with and that which he is not. It may be leaving home for the first time in his life or just doing something he has always been scared to do. However the threshold presents itself, this action signifies the Hero's commitment to his journey and whatever it may have in store for him.

Going to therapy opened up a whole new world to me. It helped me recognize that all my life I had been focused on things outside of myself, things like money, titles, material things, and other people's approval. I learned that I needed to focus my attention on what's inside of me, like my thoughts, feelings and beliefs if I truly wanted to be happy.

As a result, I became committed to understanding myself from the inside out, so I immersed myself into the study of psychology, philosophy, spirituality, and personal development.

6. Tests, Allies, Enemies

Now finally out of his comfort zone, the Hero is confronted with an ever more difficult series of challenges that test him in a variety of ways. Obstacles are thrown across his path; whether they be physical hurdles or people bent on thwarting his progress, the Hero must overcome each challenge he is presented with on the journey towards his ultimate goal.

The Hero needs to find out who can be trusted and who can't. He may earn allies and meet enemies who will, each in their own way, help prepare him for the greater ordeals yet to come. This is the stage where his skills and/or powers are tested, and every obstacle that he faces helps us to gain a deeper insight into his character and ultimately identify with him further.

After therapy, I needed to continue my growth so I began participating in a wide variety of personal development seminars. During the seminars I was challenged to address my internal fears and doubts about myself. What really helped me grow was my willingness to allow other people to support and encourage me. I learned that I had a huge issue with trust, and by being willing to work with others I learned how to trust again.

7. Approach to the Inmost Cave

The inmost cave may represent many things in the Hero's story such as an actual location in which lies a terrible danger or an inner conflict which up until now the Hero has not had to face. As the Hero approaches the cave he must make final preparations before taking that final leap into the great unknown.

At the threshold to the inmost cave the Hero may once again face some of the doubts and fears that first surfaced upon his call to adventure. He may need some time to reflect upon his journey and the treacherous road ahead in order to find the courage to continue. This brief respite helps the audience understand the magnitude of the ordeal that awaits the Hero, and escalates the tension in anticipation of his ultimate test.

After a few years of workshops and reading a few hundred books, I was at a point in my life where I was feeling pretty good about myself and I had started rebuilding my life. It hadn't been easy, but all of my hard work had paid off. My relationships were real and authentic; I felt happy and whole within myself; I had found a job that provided some financial stability; and I was pretty optimistic about my future and life in general. But despite this, something was missing. I couldn't put my finger on it, but internally I knew there was something more I needed to do.

8. Ordeal

The Supreme Ordeal may be a dangerous physical test or a deep inner crisis that the Hero must face in order to survive, or for the world in which the Hero lives to continue to exist. Whether it be facing his greatest fear or most deadly foe, the Hero must draw upon all of his skills and his experiences gathered upon the path to the inmost cave in order to overcome his most difficult challenge.

Only through some form of "death" can the Hero be reborn, experiencing a metaphorical resurrection that somehow grants him greater power or insight necessary in order to fulfill his destiny or reach his journey's end. This is the high-point of the Hero's story and where everything he holds dear is put on the line. If he fails, he will either die or life as he knows it will never be the same again.

During my journey of transformation I came upon a book by John Bradshaw that would change my life forever. The book was *Healing The Shame That Binds You* and after reading it I knew I had found the missing piece of my life's puzzle. What I learned from the book was that all my life my actions had been driven by a deep feeling of shame. It was shame that had driven me to be successful. It was also shame that kept me from creating intimacy and connection in my relationships. It was shame that kept me isolated from others and didn't allow me to truly trust anyone. It was a deep feeling of shame that kept me trapped in my own private prison and kept me from expressing who I really am.

I decided that I wanted to remove that shame and I chose to participate in a workshop with John Bradshaw called *Healing Your Inner Child*. During this workshop I learned how my abusive childhood was the source of my feelings of shame. I had to allow myself to go back and experience the pain and trauma of those earlier events in my life in order to move past the shame. During the process, I learned how the abuse I experienced caused me to disconnect from my emotions, and by allowing myself to feel them I could then begin the process of healing. This emotional healing process is what allowed me to become free of the shame. By releasing my shame and forgiving myself, I opened the door to emotional freedom and I was able to complete my life's puzzle and move forward with my life.

9. Reward (Seizing the Sword)

After defeating the enemy, surviving death, and finally overcoming his greatest personal challenge, the Hero is ultimately transformed into a new state, emerging from battle as a stronger person and often with a prize.

The Reward may come in many forms: an object of great importance or power, a secret, greater knowledge or insight, or even reconciliation with a loved one or ally. Whatever the treasure, which may well facilitate his return to the Ordinary World, the Hero must quickly put celebrations aside and prepare for the last leg of his journey.

After my experience with the inner child work, everything changed for the better. For the first time in my life I felt whole and complete. I no longer sought out exterior validation because I was happy and content with who I am as a human being. My shame was replaced with a deep self-confidence and I learned how to accept myself and love myself unconditionally. This was definitely my greatest gift - Learning to love myself just for the man that I am.

10. The Road Back

This stage in the Hero's journey represents a reverse echo of the Call to Adventure in which the Hero had to cross the first threshold. Now he must return home with his reward, but this time the anticipation of danger is replaced with that of acclaim and perhaps vindication, absolution, or even exoneration.

But the Hero's journey is not yet over, and he may still need one last push back into the Ordinary World. The moment before the Hero finally commits to the last stage of his journey may be a moment in which he must choose between his own personal objective and that of a Higher Cause.

As a result of doing my inner work I came to the conclusion that I wanted to share the lessons I learned about myself with others. Although I had no writing experience or training, I decided that I would begin writing books in the hopes to inspire others. What I have also learned is that in writing books and sharing lessons with others I continue to learn and grow. The road of life has lots of twists and turns and sometimes all we need are some guideposts along the way, and that is why I have chosen to be a writer. Writing helps me return home to my true self while guiding others to do the same.

11. Resurrection

This is the climax in which the Hero must have his final and most dangerous encounter with death. The final battle also represents something far greater than the Hero's own existence with its outcome having far-reaching consequences to his Ordinary World and the lives of those he left behind.

If he fails, others will suffer, and this not only places more weight upon his shoulders but in a movie, grips the audience so that they too feel part of the conflict and share the Hero's hopes, fears, and trepidation. Ultimately the Hero will succeed, destroy his enemy, and emerge from battle cleansed and reborn.

When I first began writing I had to face a multitude of fears. What if nobody reads my books? What if they read them and don't like them? What gives me the right to write and publish a book? Who am I to think that I can be a successful author? Since I don't have any credentials, will I be ridiculed and attacked?

All of these fears were unwarranted. By being willing to face my fears and move past any preconceived ideas I had about what it takes to be an author, I learned that I no longer needed anyone else's approval or permission to do what I love to do. I love writing! I love being an author! That's it, end of story! As a writer I simply must write because it's what's inside me. Even if I never sold a single book or no one ever reads my writings, I would still write because I have to, because it is a creative outlet that I have to express.

If I had not heeded my call to adventure I would probably still be stuck on that societal rollercoaster, and I would have never discovered my gift for writing. So all of the struggles and challenges that I overcame helped me resurrect the gift of writing that had always been sitting dormant within me.

A part of me died during this process, yet the real me was resurrected and it was worth all the pain and suffering I had endured along the way.

12. Return with the Elixir

This is the final stage of the Hero's journey in which he returns home to his Ordinary World a changed man. He will have grown as a person, learned many things, faced many terrible dangers, and even death, but now looks forward to the start of a new life. His return may bring fresh hope to those he left behind, a direct solution to their problems, or perhaps a new perspective for everyone to consider.

The final reward that he obtains may be literal or metaphoric. It could be a cause for celebration, self-realization, or an end to strife, but whatever it is it represents three things: change, success, and proof of his journey. The return home also signals the need for resolution for the story's other key players. The Hero's doubters will be ostracized, his enemies punished, and his allies rewarded. Ultimately the Hero will return to where he started, but things will clearly never be the same again.

As I reflect back over my twenty-year journey of transformation it is nothing short of a miracle. I could have never imagined the joy and gratitude I feel on a daily basis as a result of going on my own hero's journey. By accepting my own call and trusting my inner wisdom, I awakened to my own divine purpose and discovered some unique gifts and talents I have that allow me to support others in their journey. That's very rewarding and fulfilling for me. I took the road less traveled and it has made all the difference in my life and in the lives of others.

I have come to accept that the Hero's Journey isn't just a theory; it is a step-by-step process of discovering who you really are and why you are here. At some point every human being must engage in their own journey and each one is as unique as our fingerprints. No two are exactly the same.

It begins with your acceptance of a very simple fact - you are indeed a hero, and therefore you are already engaged in the hero's journey, whether you realize it or not. By becoming aware of this fact and following these 12 stages, I believe you can begin and finish your own Hero's Journey.

Rest assured that it may not be easy, but I guarantee it will be worth it.

If you're interested in going deeper, I highly recommend that you pick up a copy of Joseph Campbell's book *The Hero With A Thousand Faces*. It's a fascinating read that explains the hero's journey in more detail. If you can find the interview with Bill Moyers and Joseph Campbell, do yourself a favor and watch it!

I also recommend that you pick up a copy or watch the movie *Finding Joe* by Patrick Takaya Solomon. It is a beautiful film that illustrates how the Hero's Journey works, and has some great insights from a variety of different experts on the Hero's Journey theory.

You can also Google The Hero's Journey and get an infinite amount of information and resources to learn more.

I want to close this chapter with a quote.

> "It's not what happens to you that matters, it's how you respond to what happens to you that makes all the difference in the world."

May The Force Be With You!

"Every great man, every successful man, no matter what the field of endeavor, has known the magic that lies in these words: every adversity has the seed of an equivalent or greater benefit."

W. Clement Stone

Chapter 7
The Breakdown Breakthrough Principle

Have you ever heard of the Chinese Bamboo Tree? What makes this plant so unique is the fact that once it is planted it takes approximately five years before the seed actually breaks through the ground and becomes visible. But once the seed breaks ground, it has been known to grow more than 90 feet in less than six weeks! Some bamboo has been known to grow 8 feet (96 inches) in a 24-hour period!

Take a moment and let that sink in.

Imagine a farmer who plants the seeds and then begins waiting for the seed to grow. After the first year I'm sure he begins to get a little impatient, but because of his commitment, he continues to water and nurture the plant and he has faith that eventually the plant will grow.

After the second year I'm sure the neighbors would begin to question his sanity. They would probably watch him taking care of something that they could not see, and would probably call him crazy for putting all his energy and effort into something that has not produced any crop in more than two years.

After the third year I'm sure he would begin to question his own sanity. It would take a tremendous amount of faith to continue taking care of something for more than three years and not see a return on your investment. But the farmer intuitively knows that eventually the tree will grow, and he will reap huge rewards for his commitment and dedication, so he continues to have faith that the tree will break ground soon and therefore he keeps watering and nurturing his plants.

By the fourth year he is probably concerned that he chose the wrong plants to grow. He's probably thinking that a faster growing crop may have been a better choice, but once again he holds on to his faith and continues to believe that his plants will grow. He has a vision for his plants, and he knows that he must hold on and continue to feed and water his plant, and believe with all his heart that his plants will eventually begin to grow.

By the fifth year I'm sure he has considered giving up and planting something different. Although he is confident that his plants will eventually grow, after five years it is easy to see how he might have lost faith. But a true farmer has deep faith in his ability to grow and nurture his crops, and he holds on to that faith with the knowing that eventually his plants will begin to sprout.

Now try to imagine how he might feel after the fifth year when he finally sees the plant break the ground. Since the tree has been documented to grow up to eight feet tall in a twenty-four hour period, just imagine how excited the farmer would be as he watched his plant grow at such a rapid rate. I'm sure he would be filled with gratitude and excitement that all his hard work had definitely paid off.

This true story of the Chinese bamboo tree serves as a perfect metaphor for the Universal Law called the Breakdown Breakthrough Principle. It is a law that is irrefutable. When you fully understand how it works, you will never look at adversity the same way again.

Let's take a deeper look into the story of the Chinese Bamboo Tree and how its story applies to your life.

First of all, you must understand that everything the tree needs to be itself is already encoded inside it. It's DNA and genes make it what it is.

Next, it must be implanted into fertile ground in order to grow; the soil conditions need to be perfect in order for it to begin taking root.

Next, the seed must be nurtured and cared for to grow. It will need adequate water, nutrients, sunlight, and someone who cares enough about the plant that they are willing to do whatever it takes to help it grow.

Next, it needs time to grow a substantial root system to anchor itself deeply into the ground so that it will be strong enough to handle the phenomenal growth it will go through once it breaks through the ground. Without a strong foundational root system there is no way the plant could handle the rapid growth.

Finally, it simply needs to express all that it is. Once the plant breaks ground it's only purpose is to become a Chinese bamboo tree. It is encoded in its DNA to grow and express all that it is. There is a divine intelligence that permeates the seed that becomes the tree. It has a specific and unique code that is unlike any other plant, and therefore it expresses its unique self as a Chinese bamboo tree.

You are just like the Chinese bamboo tree!

You are born with everything you need to become the divine unique individual that you are. It is encoded in your DNA. You have everything you need right now in this very moment to create anything you desire in life. You are the master of your own fate, and it is your responsibility to claim your own destiny. You are fully equipped right now to live the life you were born to live.

Then you were born into fertile ground. No matter what situation you were born into, it is perfectly suited for you. Your environment, no matter how difficult, is exactly the right environment for you to grow in. All the conditions of your life are orchestrated by a divine intelligence that never makes mistakes. So no matter where you've begun, it is absolutely perfect for you. Your environment is the soil condition of your life, and it has everything you need in order for you to grow.

Next, you are 100% responsible for nurturing yourself in order to grow. You must make the commitment to yourself that you will nurture your emotional, intellectual, physical, and spiritual aspects of yourself. No one can do this for you - you must do this yourself. There will be times in which you must seek support from others, but only *you* can change you. You must do the nurturing yourself, and it's an inside job.

Now, all adversity and challenges you experience in life help you to develop your spiritual, psychological, and emotional root system. Have you ever heard the quote; "If it doesn't kill you it can only make you stronger?" There is a lot of truth to that statement. Adversity is simply another name for breakdown. Breakdowns are always preparation for breakthroughs. When we understand that the bigger the breakdown the greater the breakthrough, then we have the key to turning all adversities into allies.

Finally, your job is to become the grandest version of the greatest vision you have for yourself as a human being (to quote Neale Donald Walsch). You are here to express your unique gifts and talents with the world and to use those gifts to make the world a better place. But first of all, you must come to the awareness that you are a divine expression of the Infinite Intelligence that created this amazing Universe we live in. Everything you need to do this is already encoded in your DNA. Your job is to access your divinity and be willing to express it as only you can.

So I would like you to take a moment and think about your own life right now. Are you currently in breakdown? Are you experiencing adversities in your life? If the answer is yes, I hope you take some time and think about the breakdown breakthrough principle. As difficult as it might be right now. I want you to know that there are breakthroughs on the other side of your breakdowns. To support you in dealing with possible breakdowns in your life. I want to share 10 keys that will help you get through your breakdowns and towards your breakthroughs. As I've mentioned before, I've definitely had my share of breakdowns so you can rest assured that these 10 keys can definitely support you in getting through those difficult times in your life.

1. Seek support

Unfortunately, most people will not take this first step but it is absolutely imperative that you do. There is absolutely nothing wrong with seeking support. It does not make you weak; it will actually make you stronger. As soon as you commit to seeking support you begin the process of breaking through the challenges in your life.

I realize how difficult this can be. When I was going through the breakdowns in my own life I initially refused to seek support. I believed that if I just read enough books or listened to enough audio programs I could "fix" myself and eventually become happy. What I learned was that I was too ashamed and embarrassed to ask for help, and deep down I actually didn't believe that I deserved help. Fear, shame, pride, and embarrassment initially kept me from seeking support, but eventually I gained the courage to get help. These feelings can keep you from experiencing breakthroughs in your life. Don't let them! Gain the courage to seek support and I can assure you that your life will get better and easier.

Support can come from a wide variety of sources. You could try therapy or a support group. You could hire a life coach, you could seek support through a religious organization, or you could even open up to a trusted friend whom you trust and can confide in. The key is your willingness to speak with others about the breakdowns in your life and allow them to be there for you emotionally, psychologically, and spiritually as you go through them. Noted psychologist and author John Bradshaw said it best when he stated; "In order to truly heal you must be willing to create an interpersonal bridge with another human being." What he means by that is we must be willing to get out of our heads and into our hearts and allow ourselves to feel and heal. This can only be accomplished through our willingness to gain support from others.

Too many times people don't trust others or allow them to be there for them because they are too afraid or ashamed that they will be judged about things they may be afraid to admit. Do not fall into this trap. There are people who will support you and care for you if you are willing to allow them to. We have all done things we may not be proud of, but we must be willing to take the risks and know that true friends and support systems do not judge. They support you and allow you to be who you really are and they love you unconditionally. Even with all your mistakes and perceived imperfections, people can and will accept you for who you are if you are willing to allow them to do so.

So find a group of like-minded people who are on the same path as you and are willing to support you and your growth, and you will have begun to lay the foundation for dealing with all the breakdowns you will encounter in your life.

2. Choose a breakdown theme song

One of the things that truly helped me during the most difficult times of my life was listening to music. Music is a powerful way to get in touch with your emotions and it can help you deal with most challenges and difficulties in life. Choosing a breakdown theme song is an excellent way of giving yourself some tools to help you deal with the multiplicity of challenges you face on a regular basis.

The key is to choose a song that resonates with you and play it whenever you experience a breakdown. Make sure that you choose a song that you really love and relate to. It should definitely be a song that is uplifting and positive, and it should invoke feelings of happiness and success. Do not choose a song that makes you sad and reminds you of painful experiences, choose one that inspires and motivates you to break through the challenges you may be facing.

One of my favorite breakdown theme songs is *When I'm Back On My Feet Again* by Michael Bolton. During the darkest periods of my life I would listen to this song over and over again and it never failed to lift my spirits. As I listened to the song I would imagine myself moving past all the obstacles in my life and it filled me with hope and optimism. I would like to share the words to the song with you because they helped me overcome a lot of adversity in my life, and I know that the message that the song shares is very powerful and transformative.

"When I'm Back On My Feet Again"

Gonna break from these chains around me
Gonna learn to fly again
May be hard, may be hard
But I'll do it
When I'm back on my feet again

Soon these tears will all be dryin'
Soon these eyes will see the sun
Might take time, might take time
But I'll see it
When I'm back on my feet again

When I'm back on my feet again
I'll walk proud down that street again
And they'll all look at me again
And they'll see that
I'm strong

Gonna hear the children laughing
Gonna hear the voices sing
Won't be long, won't be long
Till I hear them
When I'm back on my feet again

The Breakdown Breakthrough Principle

> Gonna feel the sweet light of heaven
> Shining down its light on me
> One sweet day, one sweet day
> I will feel it
> When I'm back on my feet again
>
> And I'm not gonna crawl again
> I will learn to stand tall again
> No I'm not gonna fall again
> Cos I'll learn to be strong
>
> Soon these tears will all be dryin'
> Soon these eyes will see the sun
> Won't be long, won't be long
> Till I see it
> When I'm back on my feet again
>
> When I'm back on my feet again
> I'll be back on my feet again

If you've never had the pleasure of listening to this song I highly recommend that you do so. When you combine these amazing words with the soulfulness of the singer's voice and the beautiful instrumentals, it becomes a powerful positive inspirational theme song that will definitely uplift your spirit.

The important thing is for you to choose a song that truly resonates with you. Choose a song and listen to it so often that you actually put it to memory. You will be surprised how the song will subconsciously pop into your mind when you are stressed out or challenged. Having a breakdown theme song is a great way to turn your adversities into allies.

If you would like some suggestions on potential

breakdown theme songs, here are a few more of my favorites.

Coming Out Of The Dark by Gloria Estefan
We Fall Down by Donnie McClurkin
Never Would Have Made It by Marvin Sapp

3. Use your imagination

A great tool to use when you experience breakdown is your imagination. You must begin seeing yourself moving through the difficulties and challenges in your life. One way to do this is by creating a vision board, which consists of pictures from magazines, books, the Internet, or any other source that helps you visualize whatever it is you want. Place the pictures somewhere you can see them every day, and spend some time looking at them and imagining that you already have them.

When I was completely broke and living in a rented one-room apartment with no job or car, I began using a vision board to visualize myself putting my life back together. I placed pictures of my dream house, my dream wife, a healthy body, money in the bank, and a picture of me giving speeches to millions of people around the world. I would look at these pictures every day and I would generate the feelings I would have if they were real.

Although it didn't happen overnight, I was eventually able to overcome all the challenges I was dealing with, and I currently have a beautiful home, a wonderful wife, I've written three books (not including this one), and I host a radio show that is broadcasted to more than eight countries around the world. I've also hosted a cable television in Houston Texas that actually reached millions of people.

It all began with me using my imagination and visualizing the things I wanted and believing that eventually I would have them. I had to see and believe the images I placed in my mind and then take action to bring those things to reality. But it all began in my imagination.

Always remember, whatever the mind can conceive you can achieve if you truly believe. But you must be willing to believe and then take massive action to make things happen. They aren't going to magically appear if you don't put forth the effort.

4. Start a gratitude journal

One of the most powerful ways to get your life back on track is to begin a gratitude journal. It's actually pretty simple. Purchase a journal (or do it on your computer) and make a commitment that every day you will simply write down five things you are grateful for. That's' it! Each day, preferably at the same time, take a moment and write five things that you're grateful for. It can be as simple as:

1. I'm grateful that I have a roof over my head
2. I'm grateful that I have eyes to see
3. I'm grateful that I know how to read and write
4. I'm grateful that I watched my favorite movie today
5. I'm grateful that I had a delicious breakfast.

Only you can decide what you're grateful for, so get into the habit of writing your gratitude list and I can promise you that your life will begin to change. But you must commit to writing your list every day. There will be a part of you that will try to make excuses not to do it, but you must simply commit to it and then take Nike's advice: "Just Do It!" If you can do it for 21 days straight it will then become a habit and it will become a part of your daily routine that you look forward to and enjoy doing.

The powerful thing about the journal is that it challenges you to focus your attention on things that are going well for you, and it focuses on the positive. As you continue writing, you will continue to find more things to be grateful for and pretty soon your attitude will begin to change.

Whenever we are faced with challenges it is easy for our thoughts to focus on the negative and all the things that may be wrong with our lives, and when we focus on the negative we attract more negativity into our lives. When we begin to focus our attention on the things we are grateful for, we literally change our thinking, which then changes our actions, which ultimately changes our outcomes.

Remember this famous quote; "Accentuate the positive and eliminate the negative. Start your gratitude journal today!

5. Do something for others

Whenever you're in breakdown, a surefire way to raise your spirits and put yourself on the path to breakthrough is to do something for others. Being in service to others in some way will always make you feel better. Even when your life is in complete breakdown and it appears that you have nothing to give, there is always something you can do for others that won't cost you a thing. For example, did you know that offering a smile to a complete stranger is a way of doing something for others? Did you know that you could call up a friend and ask them if there is anything you can do to help them in any way?

There are countless ways that you can volunteer your time and talents to help others if you simply make the decision that you want to be in service. It's really that simple. Make a choice that you are going to do something of value to someone else and watch how your attitude changes.

When I was basically homeless without a job and no steady income, if I had a dollar (or sometimes even less) in my pocket I would sometimes go out and find a homeless person who was worse off than I was and I would offer them my last dollar. I gave the dollar unconditionally and didn't think about how the person was going to use it. I would simply give them the dollar and say one of my favorite prayers and sit back and watch the magic happen.

Here is my prayer: "Divine love through me blesses and multiplies all the good I am and have, all the good I give and receive." This powerful prayer of gratitude and abundance always warmed my heart and I would feel so much better as a result of serving others that no matter what my financial situation was, I felt rich. Amazingly, every time I did this something would happen and I would end up receiving a blessing in some form or another.

So whenever you're in a breakdown, consider doing

something for others and let the magic happen.

6. Find something to laugh about

When you are smack dab in the middle of a breakdown it may be extremely difficult to find something to laugh about. The truth is, that's the time when you should definitely find something that makes you laugh. Laughing may not make your problems go away, but it will definitely make it easier to deal with whatever problem you may be facing.

Watch a funny movie, listen to your favorite comic, or find a friend that makes you laugh and it will give you the strength and awareness to deal with your life challenges. Laugh often and laugh loudly - it's good for you.

7. Spend time in nature

When was the last time you walked barefoot through grass or felt a cool ocean wave splash up against your leg? Have you ever watched a beautiful sunrise or sunset and simply marveled at this amazing Universe we live in? There is something magical and healing about nature that truly soothes the soul. We live in such a fast-paced, technology-driven culture that we sometimes disconnect from the earth and nature, and then we wonder why we feel so disconnected. If you would like a way to move through breakdown periods in your life, why not try to reconnect with nature? Leave your cell phones and gadgets at home and simply spend time outside somewhere and allow yourself to reconnect with the beauty and majesty of nature.

8. Watch an inspirational movie

I love watching movies and I have come to realize that movies are simply metaphors for life and that they can help us to deal with adversity in our lives if we view them with an open heart and mind. Of course, it's important that we watch movies that inspire and uplift us instead of perpetuate all the things that may appear to be wrong with the world.

Have you ever watched a movie that made you feel really good and inspired you to look at life a little differently? Do you have a favorite movie that makes you feel that way? If you do, why not take a little time and re-watch it if you're currently in a breakdown period of your life?

If you don't have any ideas for feel-good movies, here are some of my favorites.

The Pursuit of Happyness
The Bucket List
Pretty Woman
Rudy
Dead Poets Society
Up
Remember the Titans

Each of these movies holds a special place in my heart because every time I watch them I feel good and they inspire me. I have used them countless times to help me through some breakdown periods in my own life, so I hope they will do the same for you.

9. Clear out unnecessary stuff in your life.

It's important that we do some "spring cleaning" at least once a year in all areas of our lives. It can begin with cleaning up your home and getting rid of old clothes or furniture that you no longer need, or you could clean out a closet or your garage and let go of "stuff" that you simply do not use any more.

It could also mean cleaning up all of your electronic gadgets by deleting emails and junk pictures and files that you no longer need. You can even delete old phone numbers of people that you are no longer in contact with.

The key is to "de-clutter" your life and make room for something new. So if you find yourself in a breakdown period, take some time to let go of the things you don't need and give yourself permission to bring some new things in to your life.

10. Develop a positive spiritual connection with a power greater than yourself.

This is possibly the most important step you can take to help you deal with breakdowns in your life. There are some teachings that suggest that you are born a sinner into a world of sin and you must repent of those sins before God will love and accept you. I believe nothing could be further from the truth. You are not born a sinner, and the world is not a sinful place.

You are born a divine unique human being who possibly made some bad choices in your life, and you must always accept the consequences of your choices. I do not believe that there is an angry vengeful God that is taking notes of your life and waiting for you to mess up so that He can condemn you to eternal damnation.

If you happen to believe in this type of God that

punishes and judges you for your "sins" it makes it extremely difficult to move through breakdown periods in your life. Your rationale becomes that you are a bad person and God must now punish you. You will then view your current situation as punishment, and since you believe you are a sinner, you will actually believe that you deserve the punishment.

Do not fall into this religious trap.

Rest assured that you are a beautiful expression of the Infinite Intelligence that created this Universe, and it wants nothing more than for you to become a joyful beautiful expression of who you really are. If you adopt a positive spiritual connection with a power greater than yourself, you will come to know that this power only wants the best for you. It isn't causing the breakdowns in your life - you are. Its job is to only love and support you, but you must accept that it is there for you. You do not have to be religious to come to this understanding, but you might have to challenge some of your deeply held erroneous beliefs that taught you that you are a sinner and unworthy of love.

Not only are you worthy of love, you are actually an expression of it. When you experience breakdowns in your life it really means that you have disconnected from the love that you are. Your challenge is to reconnect to the love, and one way to do this is by creating a positive spiritual connection with a power greater than yourself.

As a former Atheist I rejected the possibility that there was a power greater than myself in the Universe for several years, but after taking the time to come to my own understanding about God/Source, I must admit that it is now the driving force of my life. I will admit that I consider myself to be spiritual, not religious, because I personally believe that all religions really do teach and say the same thing. What they say is that there is a power in the Universe that all human beings have access to, and religions are supposed to help them access this power. Unfortunately, a lot of the religious texts are misinterpreted and the teachers of most religions promote the idea that their way is the only way to interpret scripture, and this is the reason religion causes so much divisiveness and separation amongst people.

So in no way am I advocating that you join a church or get attached to religious dogma and doctrine. I'm suggesting that there is a presence and a power in the Universe that you have direct access to, and it is your responsibility to develop a positive connection with it, and when you do, you will have everything you need to deal with any adversity or breakdown that shows up in your life.

These 10 keys can support you in dealing with any breakdown or adversity. Let's review them briefly before we move on to the next chapter.

1. **Seek support**
2. **Choose a breakdown theme song**
3. **Use your imagination**
4. **Start a gratitude journal**
5. **Do something for others**
6. **Find something to laugh about**
7. **Spend time in nature**
8. **Watch an inspirational movie**

9. Clear out unnecessary stuff in your life.
10. Develop a positive spiritual connection with a power greater than yourself.

Your takeaway from this chapter should be that there are always breakthroughs on the other side of breakdowns. As a matter of fact, you should recognize that the breakdowns are simply preparations for the breakthroughs - you need the breakdowns to get you ready for the breakthroughs. Rest assured that you have everything you need right now to deal with any challenge you're confronted with, you just have to make a commitment to yourself that you are willing to do whatever it takes to move through the breakdowns and then take some time to celebrate your breakthroughs.

You can do it! I believe in you!

Good luck!

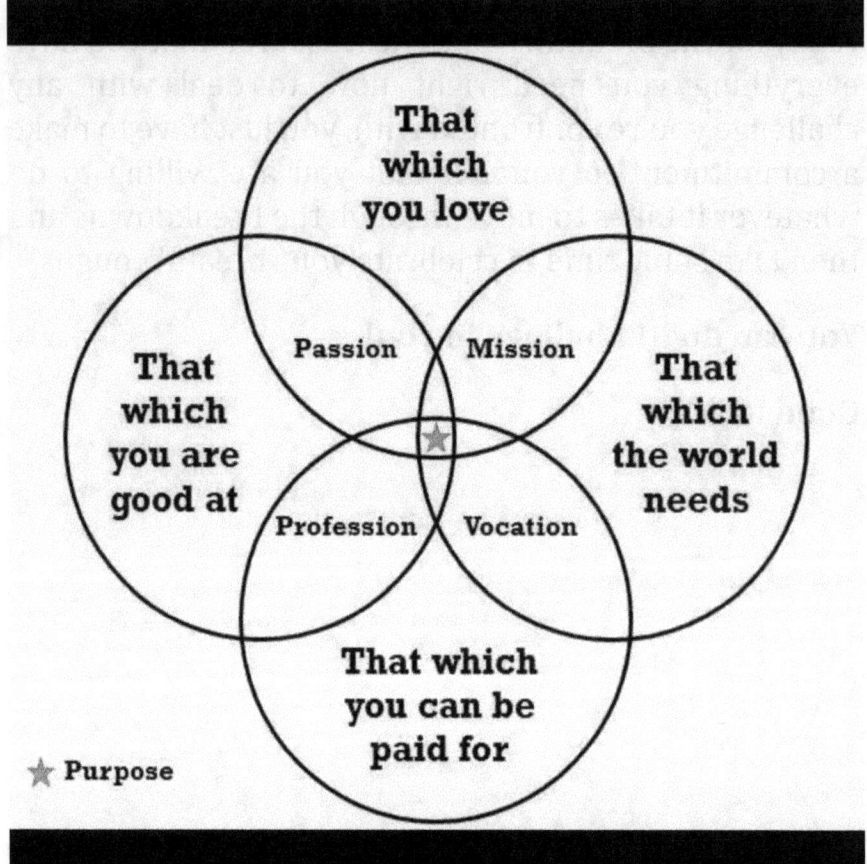

Chapter 8
The Power of Purpose

Purpose has been defined as; *"The reason for which something is done or created, or for which something exists."* I'd like to condense it and simply state, *"purpose is the reason that you have been created."* If you embrace the idea that there is The Source of all things (you can call it God, The Creator, or any other name that you're comfortable with), then try to imagine that The Source created you for a very specific purpose.

If you are truly committed to living a rewarding and fulfilling life, then I believe it is mandatory for you to discover your own unique life purpose. Without finding it, I believe something will always be "missing" from your life.

Before I share some insights on how to find your purpose, I need to begin by sharing why so few people ever find theirs. Although finding your purpose should be a high priority for all, the overwhelming majority will not take the time to discover what their purpose is.

The short and simple, yet complex reason most people never pursue nor find their purpose, is because our societal and cultural conditioning has always taught us to always look outside of ourselves for validation and fulfillment. Our media convinces us that materialism and the accumulation of "stuff" will make us happy, but ultimately this never works because happiness is an inside job and you will never experience it while looking "outside" of yourself. So the key to finding your purpose lies in your willingness to shift your awareness from looking outside of yourself to looking within yourself.

If you are familiar with the Christian teachings of Jesus he reinforced this idea by saying "seek ye first the kingdom of Heaven and all things will be given unto you." He then clarified what he meant by that statement by saying; "the Kingdom of heaven is within you." This kingdom can also be referred to as your interiority, which simply means the domain of your thoughts, feelings, and beliefs. In order to find your divine purpose you must be willing to become aware of this domain, and when you do, rest assured that you will enter the kingdom of heaven.

Although I stated, "purpose is the reason that you have been created" you must understand that purpose goes a lot deeper than this simple statement. To fully grasp and understand what true purpose really is, you must understand there are actually two components to your life's purpose. The first is your inner purpose, and the second is your outer purpose.

Your inner purpose is your true essence. It can also be described as your "beingness", which is a set of qualities and inner attributes that make you uniquely you. Being intelligent, inspirational, creative, and compassionate are all expressions of your beingness. These qualities are always consistent with you, no matter what you may be "doing".

Your outer purpose or "doingness" is how you express your inner purpose.

If you look at the graphic at the beginning of this chapter it shows exactly how to discover your outer purpose. If you begin with the top circle that says "that which you love" you have an exact starting point. In order to find your outer purpose, the first thing you have to do is figure out what you love to do.

If you go counter clockwise to the next circle, it says "that which you are good at". This is extremely important in finding your outer purpose. It must be something that you are really good at. This is where some people get confused about their purpose. Here is an example; let's imagine that you love to sing, but what happens if you have a terrible voice that no one will enjoy? More than likely it means you haven't found your life's purpose; you've simply found something that you love to do. Just because you love to do something does not necessarily mean that it is your purpose. If it is truly your purpose I can assure you that it will be something that you are really good at.

As we continue going counter clockwise, the next circle we get to says "that which you can be paid for". Getting paid for something does not necessarily mean that you are receiving money. Although there is absolutely nothing wrong with making money (and lots of it) getting paid for it means that you receive true fulfillment in doing what you love. In other words, you do what you love without the thought of compensation, but if you happen to be able to get paid for doing it that is simply an extra benefit. You aren't doing it for money, you're doing it because you love it, and when you do what you love the money will follow.

The final circle says, "that which the world needs". When you take what you love and combine it with what you are good at, and are then able to be compensated for your efforts and it somehow enriches the lives of others, you have found your true outer purpose. If you notice in the graphic, all circles overlap and meet in the middle, and that is exactly where you will find your life's purpose. If either part is missing you have not found your true life's purpose.

Now that you have some guidelines for finding your purpose, let's talk about the reasons why this is so important. In other words, why should you pursue your life's purpose?

According to Brandon Peele (Founder of EVR1 Institute and the 21 Day Purpose Challenge) finding purpose is a proven way to create a powerful, abundant, and fulfilling life. When we bring ourselves into direct relationship to our life's purpose, we transform every aspect of our lives, aligning our career, our health, and our relationships with our deepest and most satisfying truth.

Over the last 35 years, researchers have linked the discovery of our life's purpose to:

1. A vigorous, healthy, and long life.

- Live up to 7 years longer *(NIH, 1998; Carelton, 2014)*
- Maintains healthier cell structures *(UNC/UCLA, 2013)*
- Reduces overall mortality rate by 23% *(Mt. Sinai, 2015)*
- Correlated with cardiovascular, neuroendocrine and immune health *(Institute on Aging, UW-Madison, 2006)*

2. A strong mind.

- Doubles the likelihood of learning something new each day *(Gallup/Healthways, 2013)*

- Yields a 42 percent increase in the experience of contentment *(Leider/Metlife, 2009)*
- Decreases onset of Alzheimer's Disease by 240% *(Boyle/Rush, 2014)*
- Fights depression *(Journal of Clinical Psychology, 1980)*
- Decreases rates of teen depression *(PNAS, 2014)*

3. **A healthy heart.**

- Reduces death by coronary heart disease by 23% *(Mt. Sinai, 2015)*
- Reduces death rate from stroke by 72% *(Koizumi, 2008)*

4. **More profitable and rewarding careers.**

- Quadruples the likelihood of being engaged at work *(Gallup/Healthways, 2013)*
- Linked (91 percent) with a strong corporate purpose with profitability *(Deloitte, 2013)*
- Cited by global CEOs as one of the top 3 things (along with ethics and values) to focus on *(IBM, 2012)*
- Yields a 47% increase in the experience of abundance *(Leider/Metlife, 2009)*

5. **More fulfilling relationships.**

- Yields a 31% increase in the experience of feeling love *(Leider/Metlife, 2009)*
- Increases meaning in times of dissonance *(Stanford, 2014)*

6. **A more healthy, kind, tolerant, and educated society.**

- Decreases demand for health care services, as 86% of deaths and 77% of disease are due to lifestyle related factors - behaviors unaligned with purpose *(EU, 2013)*
- Increases racial tolerance *(Harvard / Cornell / Carelton, 2014)*
- Increases appetite for education *(Stanford, 2015)*
- Increases incidence of philanthropy and volunteering by 50% *(Gallup/Healthways, 2013)*

7. A more sustainable economy.

- 92% of customers will choose a product that has a higher purpose when price and quality are equal *(Nielsen, 2014)*
- 55% of customers will pay more for a product that has a higher purpose, an increase of 10% since 2011 *(Nielsen, 2014)*
- Driving corporate strategy: In 2014, "purpose", "mission" and "change the world" were mentioned 3,243 times on earnings calls, investor meetings and industry conferences, a 40% increase over 2009 *(Factiva, 2015)*
- Driving consumer behavior: 16% of US adults and 50% of EU adults make purchases with purpose *(LOHAS, 2015)*
- Driving business in the US: Social enterprise employs 10 million people, with revenues of $500 billion; about 3.5 percent of total US GDP *(Impact Investor, 2012)*
- Driving hiring: 70% of Millennials want purpose at work *(Harvard Business Review, 2014)*
- Driving conscious capitalism: Over 350 professors in social entrepreneurship from over 35 countries, with over 30 national and international competitions, 800 different articles and 200 cases used in social

entrepreneurship courses *(Wingate University, 2008)*
- Driving media: 800% more news articles about social enterprises between 2001 and 2011 *(Nexis, 2012)*

By bringing purpose into our lives, we become healthier; physically, emotionally, and cognitively. We nurture more fulfilling relationships, we create rewarding careers of impact, and we build a more just, equal, and sustainable world.

Never before in human history has the quality of human life been linked with one single task - FINDING OUR PURPOSE.

For more information about purpose and to check out the 21 Day Purpose Challenge with Brandon Peele log on to: planetpurpose.org.

Now that I have shared some scientific research to back up why you should find your purpose, I would now like to share an exercise called *15 Questions to Discover Your Personal Mission* by Tina Su. You can find her online at **thinksimplenow.com**.

~ ~ ~

15 Questions to Discover Your Life Purpose

The following are a list of questions that can assist you in discovering your purpose. They are meant as a guide to help you get into a frame of mind that will be conducive to defining your personal mission.

Simple Instructions:
- Take out a few sheets of loose paper and get a pen.
- Find a place where you will not be interrupted. Turn

off your cell phone.
- Write down the answers to each question. Write the first thing that pops into your head. Write without editing. Use point form. It's important to **write** out your answers rather than just thinking about them.
- Write quickly. Give yourself less than 60 seconds a question. Preferably less than 30 seconds.
- Be honest. Nobody will read it. It's important to write without editing.
- Enjoy the moment and smile as you write.

15 Questions:

1. What makes you smile? (Activities, people, events, hobbies, projects, etc.).

2. What are some of your favorite things you did in the past? What about now?

3. What activities make you lose track of time?

4. What makes you feel great about yourself?

5. Who inspires you most? (Anyone you know or do not know. Family, friends, authors, artists, leaders, etc.) Which qualities inspire you, in each person?

6. What are you naturally good at? (Skills, abilities, gifts etc.).

7. What do people typically ask you for help in?

8. If you had to teach something, what would you teach?

9. What would you regret not fully doing, being or having in your life?

10. You are now 90 years old, sitting on a rocking chair outside your porch; you can feel the spring breeze gently brushing against your face. You are blissful and happy, and are pleased with the wonderful life you've been blessed with. Looking back at your life and all that you've achieved and acquired, all the relationships you've developed; what matters to you most? List them out.

11. What are your deepest values? Select 3 to 6 and prioritize the words in order of importance to you.

12. What were some challenges, difficulties and hardships you've overcome or are in the process of overcoming? How did you do it?

13. What causes do you strongly believe in? Connect with?

14. If you could get a message across to a large group of people, who would those people be? What would your message be?

15. Given your talents, passions, and values, how could you use these resources to serve, to help, to contribute? (to people, beings, causes, organization, environment, planet, etc.).

Your Personal Mission Statement

> *"Writing or reviewing a mission statement changes you because it forces you to think through your priorities deeply, carefully, and to align your behaviour with your beliefs."*
>
> **Stephen Covey,** *'7 Habits of Highly Effective People'*

A personal mission consists of 3 parts:

- **What** do I want to **do**?

- **Who** do I want to help?

- What is the **result**? What **value** will I create?

Steps to Creating Your Personal Mission Statement:

1. **Do the exercise with the 15 questions above as quickly as you can.**

2. **List out action words you connect with.** Example: educate, accomplish, empower, encourage, improve, help, give, guide, inspire, integrate, master, motivate, nurture, organize, produce, promote, travel, spread, share, satisfy, understand, teach, write, and so on.

3. **Based on your answers to the 15 questions, list everything and everyone that you believe you can help.** Example: People, creatures, organizations, causes, groups, environment, and so on.

4. **Identify your end goal. How will the 'who' from your above answer benefit from what you 'do'?**

5. **Combine steps 2-4 into a sentence, or 2-3 sentences.**

~ ~ ~

Here is how I came up with my mission statement following her guidelines.

What do I want to do? Educate, motivate, and inspire.

Who do I want to help? Men.

What is the result? To support men in living extraordinary lives.

So my mission statement is to educate, motivate, and inspire men to reach their full potential and live extraordinary lives.

Take some time and complete the 15 questions, and then create your own personal mission statement. Once you do, you will then have a roadmap to help you discover and fulfill your purpose.

I must reiterate the importance of chapter 2 (Who Are You) and 3 (Make Peace With Your Past) in regards to finding your purpose. If you take the time to get to really know who you are, and then make peace with your past, I can assure you that your divine purpose will reveal itself.

I've mentioned this before and I'll mention it again. Finding your purpose will not be easy, but it will be worth it. Based on my own experience, I can honestly say that finding my purpose has been one of the most gratifying and fulfilling things that I have ever accomplished. Before I found my purpose I had no idea that I could be an author, speaker, and coach committed to serving others, but I simply made the commitment to myself that eventually I would find my purpose, and then I took massive action to make it become a reality. If I can find my purpose, so can you.

Good luck!

> *"Imagination is the beginning of creation. You imagine what you desire, you will what you imagine, and at last you create what you will."*
>
> **George Bernard Shaw**

Chapter 9
Your Heart's Desire

When I was approximately 10-years-old I specifically remember a conversation I had with my grandfather about becoming an entrepreneur. Although I had no idea what that word meant at the time, I remember telling him that one day I was going to run my own company and become very rich.

As I sit here today writing about a conversation I had more than forty years ago, I still remember the conversation as though it were yesterday. I remember feeling the dirt between my toes and the sound of farm animals cackling in the background. I remember my grandfather's loving and supportive face as he encouraged me to pursue my dream and not let anything stop me. But most importantly, I remember the feeling of confidence and the intuitive knowing that I was destined to become an entrepreneur. In my heart and soul I already knew what I wanted to do with my life, and I committed myself to live my dream and become a successful entrepreneur.

At the age of 14 I launched my first company, which put me on the fast track to fulfilling my destiny. By the time I was 17 I had built three different companies and I realized the entrepreneurial spirit was definitely encoded into my DNA.

During my junior year of high school I enrolled in a special program that allowed a student to go to school for half a day and go to work the other half of the day and receive educational credits. I loved the program because it gave me the opportunity to gain first-hand experience in the business world while making money, and I took advantage of the situation and began learning everything I could about running a business.

One of our assignments was to create a presentation that we would share with the entire class and explain where we thought our lives would be 25 years into the future. I remember taking on the assignment and being so excited that I could barely sleep as I developed my presentation in my mind and on paper.

During that same school year I had taken a career aptitude test, and based on my results it said I should become an air traffic controller. A what? An Air Traffic Controller! I have no idea how that test was devised or how it came to that conclusion, but I definitely knew that I would never even consider being an Air Traffic Controller.

I already knew exactly what I wanted to be and do with my life, and my new assignment was going to give me an opportunity to share my dream with my class. As I was preparing my presentation, I did lots of research on wealthy businessmen. One of the men that I studied was a man named Napoleon Hill. He had written a book titled *Think & Grow Rich* and it was one of my favorites. One of the great lessons from the book was called "Definiteness of Purpose". I remember having trouble pronouncing the word, but I really grasped its true meaning. I had a deep knowing in my heart exactly what I wanted to do, and I had already begun laying the foundation for becoming an entrepreneur. In other words, I had definiteness of purpose.

When the day came for my presentation I was ready. I

had done my research, studied really hard, and practiced my presentation and now it was time to share it with my class (and ultimately with the world). When it was my turn to speak, I surprised the class by changing into a custom-made t-shirt that simply had 2% on it, without explaining what it meant.

I began my presentation by sharing the conversation that I had had with my grandfather about owning my own company when I was ten. I then shared how I started my first company at the age of fourteen and how I had already started three companies so far and I was still in high school. I talked about how passionate I was about being a business man, and I even made a prediction that I would become a millionaire by the age of thirty and that I would be able to retire by the age of forty. I talked about being able to write multi-million dollar checks to charity because I believed that you should always give back once you make it to the top, and I was committed to using my money for the good of humanity. I talked about owning houses around the globe and being able to fly around in my private jet to visit them. I spoke about the high-rise building that my corporate offices would be located in and I talked about how I would create a corporate culture that created the best and brightest employees in the world.

I quoted some words of wisdom from some great business leaders and I explained to the class that I believed nothing was impossible, and that one day all my dreams would come true. When I finished, the entire class gave me a standing ovation and even the teacher said that he believed that I would accomplish all of my goals. As I was preparing to leave, I asked the students if they wanted to know what the 2% meant on my t-shirt. The majority of them said yes so I said: "The 2% t-shirt is a reminder that one day I will be in the top 2% of income earners in the country. It is a tool that I use to keep me focused and motivated."

Once again the class began applauding and I walked off feeling more confident than ever.

This occurred back in 1977 when I was seventeen years old. And to this very day it is still one of my most precious and proud moments. Although I have not reached the financial goals I projected, I can honestly say that I kept my promise to myself and followed my dream to become an entrepreneur. It was a dream that I became aware of at the tender age of ten and now here I am, some forty-four years later, and I realize that I listened to my heart and followed my dream.

I have come to believe that every human being actually has a divine dream within them. It is a specific and unique dream that each individual must discover for themselves. While some may call it a dream, I believe the more appropriate term is a heart's desire. It is a divinely inspired desire that is encoded in their DNA, and if they refuse to find it, there will always be a feeling that something is missing in their lives. No matter how much success or material wealth they attain, without discovering their heart's desire their life will not be complete.

Although every human being has a heart's desire, very few people ever find theirs. There are countless reasons why this is so, but one of the most important reasons is because we stop listening to our own hearts and begin listening to our rational minds. The reason we stop listening to our hearts is because a heart's desire is usually pretty irrational - it simply does not make sense. But when we awaken to our heart's desire it comes through as an inner knowing that defies logic, and that can be pretty scary. Some people may call it intuition, but it is knowing something without knowing how you know it. You just know it. You know it because it's in your genes. It's in every fiber of your being and it wants you to discover it. But the people who are close to you can't see it, feel it, or understand it, because it's your desire, not theirs. And they will do everything to try to protect you from pursuing it because to them it makes no sense.

Unfortunately, most people will not listen to their hearts; they listen to friends and family who will usually talk them out of their dream. The truth is, they aren't keeping you from your dream intentionally - in their mind they are protecting you because they care about you. The problem is, you start believing them and not listening to your own heart, and pretty soon they have you convinced that you shouldn't trust your heart anyway.

Since most of us are taught to be logical thinkers and to always be cautious and safe, finding your heart's desire is extremely difficult. Society will tell you to go for the American Dream, which includes the house, the wife/husband, the 2.5 kids, and the 401K and you'll be happy. Get a good education, go for a safe career that pays the most money, and you've got it made, right? Wrong! It simply does not work that way.

Have you ever noticed how many people do all of these

things and are still absolutely miserable? Why does this country have so many problems with addictions and medications? Why are so many people depressed and feel so alone? Why do 70% of people work at jobs that they hate or dislike?

It's because they haven't found their heart's desire. They haven't found their dream!

I don't want you to be one of those people. I want you to find your dream. I want you to find your heart's desire.

So I would like to share some of the lessons I've learned while pursuing my heart's desire and ultimately finding it. I'll begin by sharing one of my favorite books on the subject because it was definitely instrumental in helping me find my dream and unlocking my heart's desire. The book is *Building Your Field of Dreams* by Mary Manin Morrissey, and it is one of my all-time favorites. I highly recommend that you find yourself a copy. It is filled with incredible insights and inspiration that will lay out a step-by-step process for discovering and accessing your heart's desire.

The most powerful lesson I received from her book came to me during a time when I was basically homeless with no steady job or income and no car. Although I didn't have any material possessions, money, or titles, I had something more important. I had a dream. I knew what my heart's desire was and I had committed my life to bringing my dream to fruition. But at the time, my life was a complete mess. I was in deep debt with no way of knowing how I was going to get out of it. All the doors that I approached to help get my company started were being slammed in my face. There were times when I even questioned my sanity because everything was going wrong. At times I felt like a complete failure because I had been pursuing my dream for several years, yet nothing had materialized. A part of me wanted to give up, but another part of me knew that I could never quit.

I began reading *Building Your Field of Dreams* and I couldn't put it down. I had been following Mary Manin Morrissey online for a while and I knew her philosophy and belief system about co-creation, so when I decided to purchase her book I knew there was a lesson in it for me to learn. As I was reading the book a sentence came up that I immediately knew was the reason I had picked up the book in the first place. It was the divine message that I was supposed to hear and when I read it, I immediately recognized the special message specifically for me. It said:

"All the while you think you are building a dream but the dream is really building you." That was it, my dream was building me! It all made sense. All the time that I had spent reading books and going to seminars to learn about myself and human behavior and personal development were shaping me to become the man I was born to be. All the pain and disappointment I had overcome was actually building my faith and preparing me for something bigger and better in my life.

As a result of pursuing my dream I had become better, stronger, more confident, and my faith was stronger than ever. As I sat there accepting the divine message in her words I began to weep. I was overcome with gratitude, and in that moment felt a deep sense of connection to something greater than myself. It felt as though God/Source was sitting right next to me comforting me and letting me know that I was on the right path, and there was nothing to worry about. I then knew that everything was going to work out and that I was definitely on the right track to fulfill my heart's desire. As I sat there with tears streaming down my face, I finally experienced the beauty of the famous poem called *Footprints in the Sand*. If you have not read it, I would like to share it with you now.

> *"One night I dreamed a dream.*
> *As I was walking along the beach with my Lord.*
> *Across the dark sky flashed scenes from my life.*
> *For each scene, I noticed two sets of footprints in the sand,*
> *One belonging to me and one to my Lord.*
>
> *After the last scene of my life flashed before me,*
> *I looked back at the footprints in the sand.*
> *I noticed that at many times along the path of my life,*
> *especially at the very lowest and saddest times,*
> *there was only one set of footprints.*
>
> *This really troubled me, so I asked the Lord about it.*
> *"Lord, you said once I decided to follow you,*
> *You'd walk with me all the way.*
> *But I noticed that during the saddest and most troublesome times of my life, there was only one set of footprints.*
> *I don't understand why, when I needed You the most, You would leave me."*
>
> *He whispered, "My precious child, I love you and will never leave you.*

> *Never, ever, during your trials and testings.*
> *When you saw only one set of footprints,*
> *it was then that I carried you."*

Chasing my dream had been the catalyst of my transformation. Although I began by chasing money and material things, I had now matured enough to recognize that it wasn't about the money. It was about me following my heart's desire and becoming the entrepreneur that I had always dreamed I would become, and to become the man that I was supposed to be.

I believe this is the reason why pursuing your heart's desire is so important. When you find your heart's desire and began to believe in it and pursue it, you will be guided to grow into the person you must become in order to fully materialize your dream. Every adversity, every obstacle, then becomes an ally for you. You begin to realize that that still small voice within you will begin to whisper in your ear, and you will hear the voice of your heart's desire and it will guide you to the places you need to go to fulfill your destiny.

So, let's begin the process of locating your heart's desire.

Finding our heart's desire can sometimes be difficult because of the factors I mentioned earlier. Our rational minds will sometimes keep us from finding it. Our family and friends will also keep us from finding it, and our cultural conditioning definitely plays a part in keeping us from finding our heart's desire.

The only way you will find it is by being willing to go within and discover it for yourself. This is an inside job that only you can do, so let me begin by sharing some things to think about that may help you find your heart's desire.

Since our heart's desire is encoded in our DNA and we show up with it, a great place to start is by thinking about the things you loved to do as a child. As children, we rely more on our feelings and imaginations than we do our rational minds, and if we pay attention to what Albert Einstein once said, it lays the foundation for finding your dream. Einstein once stated that "Imagination is more important than knowledge" and I believe he was absolutely correct in this assertion. When you search for your heart's desire there is a very good chance that it may seem irrational that you can accomplish it. A part of you will say that it isn't possible, while another part of you will say that it is possible. It's like having two sets of voices in your head. One I will call your rational mind, and the other I will call the voice of your Soul.

Your rational mind is the knowledge you've received from studying and observation, while the voice of your Soul comes from a much deeper and Divine place. The voice of your Soul is creative and unlimited. It is only limited by your imagination and your imagination is limitless.

So take a moment and think back to when the Wright brothers decided to create an airplane. Can you imagine how irrational that would have sounded back in their day? I'm sure their rational mind began trying to convince them that it wasn't feasible for man to fly, but the voice of their Soul said something different. It said that it was definitely possible for them to create an airplane, so they listened to that voice and look what happened. Airplanes, space shuttles, Mars Rovers, were all created because two men decided to listen to the voice of their Souls and pursue their heart's desire.

Believe it or not, you are no different than the Wright brothers. You have a Soul voice within you that is constantly trying to get your attention. As a matter of fact, I believe it is your Soul voice that inspired you to read these words right now.

Do you remember pretending to be something as a little kid that really excited you? For me, I would pretend that I was a businessman and that I was negotiating multi-million dollar business deals in my multi-million dollar company. I even had a secret place in a wooded area close to my home where I would hold these pretend business meetings.

So what about you? Do you remember pretending to be a doctor, a rock star, a fireman, an athlete, an artist, a celebrity, or an entrepreneur? As you remember what you pretended to be, do you feel a sense of excitement inside yourself? Did thinking about it make you smile?

Or maybe you can't remember pretending to be anything as a child, maybe you currently have daydreams of something you'd like to become or something you'd like to have. Daydreams can actually be communications from your Soul that are trying to help you find your heart's desire, so it's important to pay attention to them because they just might be showing you what your heart's desire really is.

So, the first step in finding your heart's desire is to

answer this simple, yet powerful and difficult question; "What Do You Want?"

As simplistic as it may sound, most people cannot answer this question because it's actually a lot deeper than most people realize. On the surface people will say that they want to make more money, or they want to find their soul-mate, or maybe they want a new house or a new car. But if you are willing to go a little deeper, what you should find is a heart's desire that is wanting to be expressed through you.

Here is a simple exercise that can assist you in locating your heart's desire. I want you to complete this sentence;

I want.......

The key is to write down the first thing that comes to mind, no matter how irrational or absurd it may seem. Don't think too hard about it, just start free flowing whatever thoughts come to mind. Do not sensor it, just let the thoughts flow. Just keep writing until the ideas stop. If you need more space, get a separate piece of paper.

I want _____
I want _____
I want _____
I want _____
I want _____
I want _____
I want _____
I want _____
I want _____
I want _____

Once you've finished, take some time to see if any of the things on your list happen to be something you may have pretended to be, or pretended to have when you were a child. If so, pay close attention to that. Also notice how you feel as you review the list. If something stirs in you and you feel really excited about a specific thing on your list, you may have found your heart's desire.

Unfortunately this isn't an exact science, and it may take some time to find your heart's desire. But if you commit to making lists of the things you truly want, and then listen to the voice of your Soul for the answer, then there is a very good chance that you will ultimately find what you are looking for. Stick with it until you do.

Once you find something that you believe is your heart's desire then you have to put it through the Mary Manin Morrissey *Five Essential Questions Test* to confirm that it's the right one.

I can assure you that if your dream passes these five questions you are definitely ready to pursue it as your heart's desire. Here are the five questions that you must answer to determine if you've found the right dream.

1. **Does this dream enliven me?**
2. **Does this dream align with my core values?**
3. **Do I need help from a higher source to make this dream come true?**
4. **Will this dream require me to grow into more of my true self?**
5. **Will this dream ultimately bless others?**

When I first read her book I immediately asked myself these five questions. As previously mentioned, I was completely broke without knowing how I was going to manifest my dream, but I intuitively knew that somehow I was going to make my dream come true. As I answered these five questions it confirmed for me that I was on the right track and it filled me with excitement and expectancy that I would fulfill my destiny.

Here are some of the insights I received when I asked myself these five questions about my dream.

1. Does this dream enliven me?

Whenever I would think about my dream I would light up like a Christmas tree inside. There was a passion and an energy that would surge through me at the mere thought of fulfilling my heart's desire. Even to this day, being an entrepreneur excites me and fulfills me in ways that cannot be explained in words. It's been said that if you do what you love, you'll never have to work a day in your life, and I can definitely verify this statement. I absolutely love being an entrepreneur, author, and motivational speaker.

As an author, writing is my passion. It is something that is in me. I literally *have* to write. While I am writing I enter this amazing flow of energy that I can't explain in words. Athletes call it being "in the zone" and it is something that is almost magical that defies description. As an entrepreneur I am constantly challenged to ask myself deeper questions about how to run and improve my business. Though this can be challenging, it's one of the reasons I love it so much. I love the challenge! I am challenged to constantly grow and be creative in finding ways to make sure my business succeeds.

As you think about your heart's desire or dream, ask yourself honestly if it lights you up from the inside out. Does it make you to want to get up in the morning? Does the thought of it excite you? The key is to be in touch with how you feel. When you find your heart's desire you will be filled with passion and energy that will become the driving force of your life. So if you do not feel this type of excitement and energy for your dream, you have probably not found your heart's desire.

2. Does this dream align with my core values?

Knowing what your values are is extremely important. Our values are the foundation of how we interact with the world, and they will definitely affect how we express our heart's desire. If you are unclear on your values it will be difficult to know when you've found your heart's desire. If your values include honesty, openness, fairness, and integrity, then your heart's desire will reflect those values. It's important that you are clear on your values before you seek out your heart's desire.

Imagine that someone says they share the values that I mentioned. They then decide that their heart's desire is to create a company that sells illegal drugs. Well, if their core values included honesty and integrity, do you think they would have chosen a company that does not embrace the values of honesty and integrity? Clarifying your values and making sure that your heart's desire aligns with those values are paramount to your success, so make sure that you're clear on your values and align those values with your heart's desire.

3. Do I need help from a higher source to make this dream come true?

You do not have to adhere to any religious dogma or doctrine to accept that there is a power greater than yourself that can support you in fulfilling your heart's desire. As a former Atheist I can understand if you have some resistance to this particular step. What I have come to know is that there is a power greater than myself in the Universe. This power goes by lots of different names, but ultimately the name is irrelevant. What's important is that you develop a relationship or connection with it if you truly want to find your heart's desire. Ultimately, you will have to rely on it to support you in finding and ultimately manifesting your heart's desire.

There is a wonderful quote that says, "If your dream doesn't frighten you then it's simply not big enough." Having a connection to a power greater than yourself will help you to move through your fears and will ultimately give you the courage, strength, patience, and perseverance to bring your dream to fruition. If you don't need assistance I can assure you that you have not found your heart's desire.

4. Will this dream require me to grow into more of my true self?

This is the true litmus test to see if you've found the right dream. As I mentioned earlier, all the while you think you are building your dream, the reality is your dream will be building you. If you do not have to grow to build your dream, then you are chasing the wrong one. Your dream will definitely take you out of your comfort zone, and that is one of the reasons you have the dream in the first place. Too many people stay trapped in their comfort zones and they are unwilling to get out of them. They are too afraid and unsure of themselves, so they play it safe and buy into the status quo.

My suggestion is for you is to get comfortable with being uncomfortable. There can be no growth without discomfort, so you may as well accept it. If your dream does not cause you to feel uncomfortable, it's definitely not your heart's desire.

This diagram is a great representation of what you can expect when you begin pursuing your heart's desire.

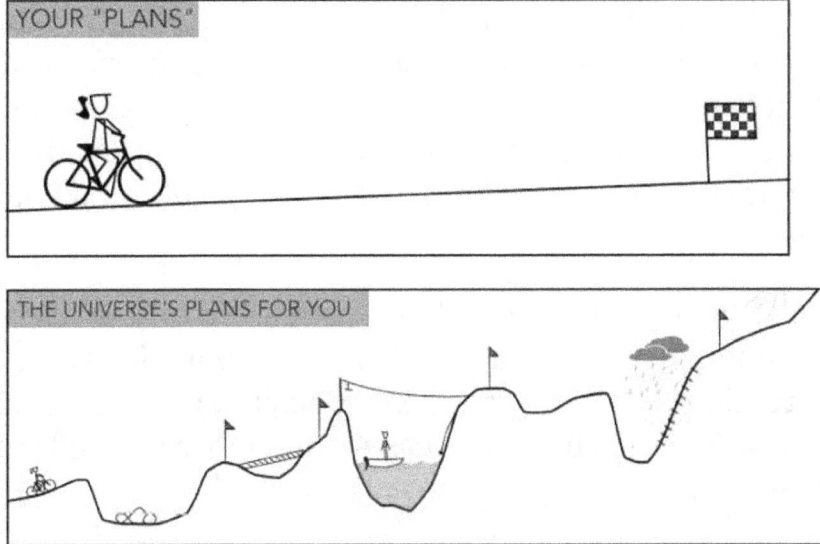

DOGHOUSEDIARIES

5. Will this dream ultimately bless others?

Muhammad Ali once said "Being in service to others is the rent we pay for our room here on earth." This powerful quote speaks to the importance of using our heart's desire to help make the world a better place. I personally believe that every human being has unique gifts and talents that are given to them to move humanity forward, and finding your heart's desire will unleash those gifts. When your dream blesses others then you know that you've found your heart's desire.

Finding your heart's desire does not have to be some grandiose experience that impacts the entire world on a large scale. Finding your heart's desire means you have found that special contribution that only you can make to the world. In your own unique way, you have had a positive impact on someone's life other than your own.

Your heart's desire could be as simple as baking pies for homeless people or teaching someone in your neighborhood to read. It does not have to be something that is featured in the headlines. It is simply something that you give from your heart unconditionally to another human being that makes them feel cared about and loved.

So instead of trying to figure out how to get rich or accumulate more material possessions, focus your attention on finding your heart's desire and I assure that you will be rich beyond measure and more fulfilled than you can even imagine.

Of course, there is absolutely nothing wrong with making lots of money and having nice things. Just make sure that you find your heart's desire and do your part in making the world a better place, and everything else in your life will fall into line.

Good luck!

"Joy, rather than happiness, is the goal of life, for joy is the emotion which accompanies our fulfilling our natures as human beings. It is based on the experience of one's identity as a being of worth and dignity."

Rollo May

Chapter 10
Living with Joy

There are some cultures that believe when you die your soul immediately goes to heaven and you are met at the entrance by angels. In order to gain entrance you must be able to answer two questions. The first question is; "Have you found joy in your life? The second question is; "Have you brought joy to others?"

So I'd like to begin this chapter by asking you the same questions. Have you found joy in your life? Take a moment and think about it.

Before you answer, I believe it's important for you to define joy. For me, joy and happiness are not the same thing. Happiness is a feeling that we experience on a regular basis as a result of being content or satisfied with something. A new car or getting a promotion can make us feel happy. It is a common emotion that makes us feel good inside and causes us to smile.

On the other hand, joy is much deeper than happiness. In some ways, joy is happiness amplified. It is an internal energy that resides deep within your soul, and when you access it your entire being lights up and radiates from within. If you've ever experienced true joy you will understand that it is difficult, if not impossible, to explain it in words because it is actually spiritual and not physical.

One day I was meditating out in nature and I was reflecting on my twenty-year journey of personal development. I had overcome a lot of adversities in my life and I was feeling extremely grateful that I had been able to put my life back together. As I sat there in deep self-introspection, I noticed that I began to smile because I was really proud of myself for overcoming so many challenges in my life. All of a sudden, I felt this deep feeling of joy arising from within me. It started out as a feeling of happiness, but it then intensified to something much, much deeper. As I allowed this feeling to arise within me I was overwhelmed by a joy that was so deep and so intense that the only thing I could do was to cry with joy. In that moment I felt a deep sense of love and gratitude for life, and it expressed itself as joy. It was such an amazing feeling that I literally sat there and cried for twenty minutes.

Without question it is absolutely possible for anyone to experience deep levels of joy. It doesn't have to be as intense as my experience, but it is a feeling that is available for anyone who simply chooses to experience it.

So what about you? Have you experienced joy in your life? Have you ever had an experience with joy that brought you to tears? Would you like to?

My experience has taught me that very few people have ever experienced true joy. That is one of the reasons why I wrote this book. I wanted to share the lessons I've learned over the past twenty years that has allowed me to experience deep levels of joy on a regular basis. This book is actually a step-by-step guide that I have used to access my inner joy, and if you follow the guidelines contained within, you too can experience true joy for yourself.

So what's the key to finding and accessing your joy? Let

me explain it by walking you back through the chapters of this book.

Chapter 1 - Adversity

It's important that we understand that life is filled with adversity. You can neither deny nor avoid this fact. More importantly is how we view adversity when it shows up in our lives. If we change our beliefs and thoughts about adversity from something that is "bad" to something that simply happens, it gives us new insights on how we can overcome all the challenges in our lives. If we face adversity with an open heart and mind, we will find that every adversity contains a lesson that can actually guide us to finding joy.

Chapter 2 - Who Are You

When we accept the truth that we are spiritual beings having a human experience rather than human beings having a spiritual experience, it allow us to see the world from a completely different perspective. When we accept our threefold nature of spirit, mind, and body, it provides us with the knowledge that we are much more than just flesh and bones. Coming to the understanding that we are actually divine expressions of The Source allows us to remove some of the erroneous teachings, such as we are sinners who are born in sin. Once we embrace who and what we really are we have laid the foundation for experiencing true heartfelt joy.

Chapter 3 - Make Peace with Your Past

It is absolutely imperative that we engage in our emotional, psychological, and spiritual healing. Healing our wounds from our past gives us direct access to joy. As long as we have unresolved emotional conflict and pain in our hearts we can never experience our joy. Healing our hearts is the key to finding joy.

Chapter 4 - Intuition/Synchronicity

Once we heal our hearts it gives us access to that still small voice within. That voice is our higher self, or the voice of The Source, and when we learn to listen to it and trust it, it will guide us to joy. When we align ourselves with that inner voice of intuition we will experience divine guidance and insights that show up in a multiplicity of ways that our minds will not comprehend. When we learn to listen to the voice of our own souls, it will always guide us to our highest good. Intuition and faith work hand-in-hand. It is the evidence of things unseen which our intuition knows how to guide us to. It may not make sense to our minds, but our hearts and souls will definitely know what to do.

Chapter 5 - Cultural Conditioning/Programming

Understanding how our mind works like a computer lets us understand that we can change our programming at any given time. We do not have to remain victim to social programming and conditioning. We can choose to change the programming that doesn't serve us and replace it with programming that does. If we don't go within and change the programming, we can rest assured that we will go without finding the joy that lies within.

Chapter 6 - The Hero's Journey

Every human being is on a divine journey. Contrary to what you may believe, your journey is absolutely perfect. No matter where you are in life right now, the key to getting and keeping your life on track is to embrace the journey and learn as much as you can about yourself along the way. There are no accidents! Despite what you may be experiencing right now, your life is absolutely perfect. How do I know this? Because results don't lie. You are where you are in life based on a series of choices you have made. If you are not happy with where you are, then you must begin by making better choices. The purpose of the journey is to guide you back home to who you really are. When you embrace and accept the journey and take complete responsibility for the choices you have made, you will learn that you must always accept the consequences of your choices, because the only person making those choices is you.

Chapter 7 - The Breakdown Breakthrough Principle

There is always chaos before creation. This is a universal law. Put another way, there is always breakdown before breakthrough. If we are willing to look deep enough we will find that every breakthrough is always preceded by a breakdown. When we come to the understanding that a breakdown is actually preparation for breakthrough, it makes it easier to embrace this universal principal. A perfect metaphor for this is the transformation of the butterfly. When a caterpillar enters into the cocoon, its entire body goes into complete breakdown. It has imaginal cells that begin eating away at the cells of the caterpillar to make room for the new cells of the butterfly. In some ways it appears to be a violent and destructive process that is killing the caterpillar, when in reality, it is a perfectly designed process by The Source that allows the butterfly to emerge from a seemingly destructive event. From chaos to creation, and from breakdown to breakthrough, is a law that is irrefutable. Every breakdown you face in life is simply preparation for a breakthrough to joy if you keep an open mind.

Chapter 8 - The Power of Purpose

Every human being shows up with a divine purpose encoded in their DNA. Not only do they show up with purpose, they also show up with everything they need to fulfill that purpose. You have everything you need right now to fulfill your purpose, but you must first discover your unique gifts and talents that were given to you by The Source. When you are able to use your gifts and talents to help make the world a better place then you have connected to your purpose.

Chapter 9 - Your Heart's Desire

When Dr. Martin Luther King Jr. declared that he had a dream he was speaking of his heart's desire. Your heart's desire is a special assignment given to you by The Source and it is your responsibility to find out what it is. If you fail to find it, something will always be missing in your life and the chances of you finding true authentic joy will be greatly reduced. It doesn't mean that you can't find joy without your heart's desire, it really means that if you want to experience joy at its deepest most intimate level possible then finding your heart's desire will definitely get you there.

When you do find your heart's desire your joy becomes the fuel that drives you forward. It ignites the passion within you that gives you faith, patience, perseverance, and persistence. It is the source of high-octane motivation and once you experience it you will have everything you need to overcome any obstacle that may be keeping you from your heart's desire.

Chapter 10 - Living with Joy

And now we are back to where we began this chapter - living with joy! Now that you've had a recap of the contents of the book can you see how it can serve as a guide to finding your joy? Each chapter covers a specific topic that should help you look deep within yourself to find your joy. It may not be easy to do, but I can promise you it will be worth it when you find it. Joy is actually your birthright, and if you aren't experiencing it right now then it's letting you know that you have some work to do. My hope is that the contents of this book can support you in some way, but ultimately it's all up to you. This book can't change your life, but you can. This book can only provide you with some tools that can help you change your life, but you must be willing to learn how to use the tools and apply them to your own life.

The second question I asked was "Have you brought joy to others?" If the answer is no, then your journey is not complete. Muhammad Ali once said "being in service to others is the rent we pay for our time here on earth" and I completely concur with his statement. Bringing joy to others actually enhances our joy. What you give you receive, so by sharing joy you receive it.

I would now like to share some joy with you by sharing

my top 10 things I do to experience and express joy in my own life. Take some time and contemplate these 10 things and make it a point to incorporate them into your daily life.

1. Know thyself

Socrates once said "Know thyself" and I believe they are words to live by. Unfortunately very few people will take the time to truly understand who they are and why they are here. Everything begins with you. If you truly want to experience joy and have a fulfilling and rewarding life, you must put forth the effort to know thyself. I have shared some ways to do this throughout this book and my hope is that you will take these things to heart and apply them to your life. A good exercise for you to assist in this process is by writing down a SWOT analysis of yourself. SWOT is an acronym for Strengths-Weaknesses-Opportunities-Threats. Simply get a piece of paper and make a list of all of your strengths, weaknesses, opportunities for growth, and the threats to your well-being. It could look like this;

My strengths. I am intelligent, creative, patient, caring, ambitious.

My weaknesses. I'm not good at seeking support, I overthink too many things, I tend to isolate myself too much.

My opportunities. Are to seek support more, engage more with others, trust my heart more, and not my head.

My threats. If I isolate myself I miss out on creating

intimate relationships with people, which will cause me to be lonely.

The key is to simply write as many of these things down as you can come up with. Keep the list handy and write more things as they come up for you. The key is awareness. You cannot change anything you're not aware of, so making this list will help you see parts of yourself that you may want to change or improve.

2. Grow thyself

Anthony Robbins declared that the key to true success is constant and never-ending improvement. This means we must make the commitment to ourselves that we are constantly learning new things and expanding our awareness. The reason this can be so challenging is because most people are stuck in their comfort zones and are too afraid to be uncomfortable. The problem is, everything you truly want and need will always be just outside of your comfort zone. In order to get something you've never had, you must be willing to do something you've never done. As a human being you have an infinite capacity for learning. In other words, there is no such thing as learning too much. So commit to growing thyself and you will have a solid foundation on which to build your remarkable life.

3. Share thyself

Be sure that you are sharing yourself with others in some way. It can be with your spouse, your children, your co-workers, or a stranger walking down the street. Sharing yourself means you can provide a helping hand for someone in need, or it could mean that you are willing to simply listen to someone with an open heart and mind and give them your full, undivided attention. It could even be as simple as sincerely smiling at a stranger and saying a little prayer for them as you walk by. No gesture is too small if you sincerely want to share yourself with others.

4. Take good care of thyself

Taking good care of thyself means that you are taking care of your emotional, intellectual, physical, and spiritual aspects of your life. A very important aspect that people neglect is the physical one. It is important that you pay close attention to your body and understand what works best for it. This means avoiding illegal drugs and substances that hurt your body, and it also means eating healthy food that contributes to your physical well-being. Exercising should be an important part of your lifestyle and you should make a commitment to get a physical at least once a year. Minimize your alcohol intake (or eliminate it) and be sure never to over indulge.

5. Embrace the silence

One of the greatest gifts that I have ever given myself is learning to meditate. Meditation has tons of benefits and absolutely no cost. However, it can be challenging and difficult to commit to and stick with. By embracing the silence and committing to meditation you gain access to deep inner peace and relaxation. Once you commit to it you also gain access to your intuition and your creativity.

The key is to simply learn how to quiet the mind so that

you can hear the voice of your own soul. You may not be aware of this, but you do have direct access to The Source through meditation. There are two things that are consistent in every major religion of the world; prayer and meditation. Prayer can be defined as speaking to God, while meditation can be defined as listening to God. You do not have to follow any rigid dogma or doctrine to speak and listen to the Divine. All you need is a commitment to doing it. So embrace the silence and experience serenity and inner peace.

6. Develop an intimate relationship with a power greater than yourself.

God goes by many different names and is worshipped in many different ways. From my perspective there are many paths to God, and just because someone may be on a different path than I am it does not mean that they are the ones who are lost. Instead of insisting that your God is the right God, or that your people are the chosen people, my suggestion is for you to simply find the path that works for you and follow it.

The key isn't whether or not your God is the right God; the key is whether or not you've chosen the right God for yourself. When you create an intimate connection with a power greater than yourself you will never have to debate or argue about your God. Throughout this book I have defined God as The Source, which really works for me. I have chosen to identify with the Divine through this description, but in truth it really does not define God as I understand it, although it comes close to expressing my deepest held beliefs about the Creator of the Universe.

The key is to find your own truth and do not simply accept someone else's truth out of duty and obligation. Go on your own journey and find the path that works for you, and you can create a connection that can never be broken.

7. Create a deep reverence for Nature

Have you ever watched a documentary about the Universe and just marveled at the awesomeness and complexity of it all? Have you ever held a newborn baby and become overwhelmed with the pure beauty and perfection of childbirth? Have you ever watched a sunrise or sunset and experienced a deep sense of reverence and connection with everything? Have you ever noticed how human beings can rally together and show deep love and compassion for each other, regardless of their ethnicity or religious beliefs when faced with devastating tragedy? Have you ever been out in nature and felt the majesty and beauty of creation that literally brought you to tears?

If we're willing to look close enough, there are lots of reasons for us to feel optimism and gratitude for this amazing gift called life. Contrary to our negative media, I believe that there are a lot more things that are right with this world than things that are wrong with it. The key is recognizing what you focus your attention on the most. You will always find what you're looking for. When we constantly focus our attention on what is wrong, we miss out on the beauty of the things that are right. Wayne Dyer said it best when he said, "If you change the way you look at things, the things you look at will change." So let me suggest that you change the way you look at the world for a moment and allow yourself to see some things that are actually right with it.

So every now and then it's a good idea to go out in nature and drink in some of its beauty. Leave the cell phone and technology at home, take off your shoes and feel the grass between your toes and listen to the birds sing and watch the squirrels play. Leave all of your problems at home and for a brief moment be fully present to your surroundings and let nature kiss you with its beauty.

8. Laugh often

When was the last time that you laughed until you cried? If you truly want to experience joy, make time for laughter and fun. Being childlike is a great way to put you in contact with your joy and laughter. This means that you stop taking things so seriously and you can learn to look at the bright side of things. Watch a funny movie, go to a comedy show, look in the mirror and simply laugh at yourself, or read a funny comic strip. These are just a few things you can do to laugh at, so what are you waiting for? Go and laugh right now. It's perfectly fine if you do. Laugh now and laugh often.

9. Embrace the mystery

If you truly want to be happy and experience true joy, I believe it is extremely important to embrace the mystery of life. It's okay not to know everything, and we definitely do not have to always be right about our points of view. Being open minded and embracing the mystery gives us the freedom to learn new things and change our perspectives. When we do this, it can ultimately lead us to new discoveries about ourselves and the world around us. As soon as we believe we know everything and become closed minded, we close the door to mystery and our life ceases to grow.

Embrace the mystery. Question everything. Be a seeker. Being open minded does not mean that your brains will fall out. Experience different cultures, try a different religion, eat some exotic food. Life was meant to be lived fully, so be open to trying different things and embrace the mysteries of life.

10. Express your creativity

Believe it or not, you are creative. Different people will obviously express their creativity differently, but the truth is every human being is creative. The challenge for you is to find your creative outlet and then go out and create something. Creativity can show up through cooking, drawing, building, singing, writing, or even through serving others. You are responsible for finding and expressing your creativity. A great way to find your creativity is by knowing out what you love to do. When you find what you love to do, your creativity will naturally follow. So how do you find out what you love to do? Here are three ways to know if you're doing what you love.

1. You will do it without the thought of compensation. In other words, you do it for the pure joy of it, and you aren't concerned with whether or not you will benefit from it in any way. Your joy is its own reward, and you're doing it simply because you love to.

2. When you are doing it you lose track of time. When

you are doing what you love, time literally disappears. You become so engaged in what you're doing that time just flies by.

3. When you are doing what you love, you want to share it with others. Expressing your creativity with others brings you joy.

So, what do you love to do? Are you expressing your creativity? If not, now is a great time to begin. Express your creativity and I can assure you that you will experience joy.

So there you have it - my top 10 things I do to experience and express joy in my own life. Are you willing to do them for yourself so that you can experience joy? The ball is now in your court, and it is completely up to you. Take Nike's advice and Just Do It!

Now we are at the end of our journey together, and I hope that the contents of this book has provided you with some insight and information to help you overcome any adversity in your life. As mentioned, life is full of adversity and it is your responsibility to turn your adversities into allies and use them as stepping-stones to live the life of your dreams. No, it won't be easy, but it's possible.

I want to leave you with a quote that truly summarizes my intention with this book. It is a quote that I live by and I use it as a guiding principle of my life. If you fully grasp its message and meaning, I can assure you that your life will be transformed.

> *"If you had one goal, and that was to feel good, you would never again need to hear another word from*

anyone. You would live successfully and happily and in a way of fulfilling your life's purpose ever after."

Abraham-Hicks

That's it! Commit to feeling good and expressing joy and you will live successfully and happily for the rest of your life.

Good luck!

Coach Michael Taylor

Resources

Coach Michael Taylor websites:

coachmichaeltaylor.com
blackmenrock.net
anewconversationwithmen.com
creationpublishing.com
blogtalkradio.com/ancwm (radio show)
twitter.com/coachmichaelt
facebook.com/coachmichaeltaylor
linkedin.com/in/coachmichaeltaylor

Recommended readings

The Seat of the Soul by Gary Zukav
A New Earth by Eckert Tolle
The Spontaneous Fulfillment of Desire by Deepak Chopra
A Return to Love by Marianne Williamson
Conversations with God by Neale Donald Walsch
Live Your Dreams by Les Brown
Spiritual Liberation by Michael Bernard Beckwith
The Biology of Belief by Dr. Bruce Lipton

Online resources for growth

purposeplanet.org
theoptimist.com
cwgportal.com
marymorrissey.com
landmarkeducation.com
tut.com
deepakchopra.com
drwaynedyer.com

About the Author

Coach Michael Taylor is an entrepreneur, author, motivational speaker and radio show host who has dedicated his life to empowering men and women to reach their full potential. He knows first-hand how to overcome adversity and build a rewarding and fulfilling life and he is sharing his knowledge and wisdom with others to support them in creating the life of their dreams.

He is no stranger to adversity and challenges. He was born in the inner city projects of Corpus Christi Texas to a single mother with six children. Although he dropped out of high school in the 11th grade, his commitment to living an extraordinary life supported him in defying the odds.

With persistence, patience and perseverance he was able to climb the corporate ladder of success and become a very successful mid-level manager of a multi-million dollar building supply center at the tender young age of 22.

After approximately eight years, he was then faced with another set of challenges as he experienced the pain and humiliation of divorce, bankruptcy and foreclosure and found himself contemplating suicide.

Bankrupt and alone, he committed to rebuilding his life which propelled him to begin a 15 year inner journey of personal transformation which resulted in him discovering his true self and his passions for living. As a result, he is now happily married (13 years) and living his dream of living an extraordinary life while being in service to others. Through his books, lectures and radio program he now coaches others on how to become genuinely happy with their lives and live the lives they were born to live.

www.ingramcontent.com/pod-product-compliance
Lightning Source LLC
Chambersburg PA
CBHW050635300426
44112CB00012B/1808